Mini Felt Christmas

First published in 2017

Search Press Limited
Wellwood, North Farm Road,
Tunbridge Wells, Kent TN2 3DR

ISBN: 978-1-78221-497-7

Suppliers

If you have difficulty in obtaining any of the materials and equipment mentioned in this book, then please visit the Search Press website for details of suppliers:
www.searchpress.com

You are invited to view the author's work at:
etsy.com/shop/sachiyoishii
visit her website at: knitsbysachi.com
visit her blog at: knitsbysachi.wordpress.com
search for KnitsbySachi on www.ravelry.com
or search for Knits by Sachi on Facebook

Printed in China through Asia Pacific Offset

Dedication
To my Mum.

Acknowledgements
Many thanks to all at Search Press, especially Katie French for being so enthusiastic about my idea for a festive felt book, Sophie Kersey for editing, Juan Hayward for his excellent design work and Paul Bricknell for the beautiful photography.

Sachiyo Ishii

Mini Felt Christmas

30 decorations to sew for the festive season

Search Press

Contents

Introduction 6
Materials & tools 8
Using the templates 11
Embroidery stitches 12
Making the dolls 14
Making animals 18

Christmas Tree Decorations 20

Embroidered baubles 22
Christmas pudding 24
Gingerbread man 25
Christmas stockings 26

Dove 28
Angel 29
Toy soldiers 30
Snowman 32
Teddy bear 33
Robin 34
Pink rabbit 35
Penguin 36
Woodland fairies 38

Santa Claus 40

Santa 42
Sleigh 44
Reindeer 46

Embroidered baubles

Christmas pudding

Gingerbread man

Christmas stockings

Dove

Angel

Toy soldiers

Snowman

Teddy bear

Robin

Pink rabbit

Penguin

Yule Log 48

Display stand 48
Chocolate log 50
Decorations 52

Gingerbread House 54

House 56
Biscuits, cookies & decorations 58
Hansel & Gretel 68
Fir tree 70

Holly Wreath 71

The Christmas Story 78

Mary & Joseph 80
Jesus 81
Shepherds 82
Kings 84
Animals 87
Camels 90

Templates 92

Woodland fairies

Santa

Sleigh

Reindeer

Yule log

Gingerbread house

Fir tree

Hansel

Gretel

Holly wreath

Mary & Joseph

Shepherds

Kings

Animals

Camels

Introduction

When I was in year 5 at primary school, one of my classmates brought a little felt mascot doll to school. She had made it all by herself. It hung from her school bag and looked very charming. I was very impressed by her creation and also amazed that someone as young as I was could make such a lovely thing. I told her I would love to have one just like it but instead of making another one for me, she lent me her instruction book the next day. I quickly fell in love with the book and dashed to a craft shop to buy some felt squares with my pocket money. I bought one in black and one in white, and my very first project was a little panda.

Sewing mascots became a trend in our class and everyone started making felt dolls and animals. We bought more books from the same author and took turns learning and copying the templates. We exchanged the end results as gifts for Christmas. I gave one doll to a boy I had a crush on, and luckily he really liked it!

I guess this is how my love for craft started at the age of ten. Unfortunately, I became too busy with school work and the constant pressure of keeping grades up, so my life as a crafter ended up being put away and forgotten until I became a mother. In Japan, we have a proverb: 'The spirit of a three year old persists until the age of 100'. Our traits and personalities as children do not change as we get older, so luckily I rediscovered the joy of craft.

During the creation of this book, I often thought about my happy memories with felt. It was the perfect material for a young beginner like me. Felt squares are relatively inexpensive, widely available and easy to handle. You can't go wrong, so why not have a go?

If you are not confident with a sewing machine, all the projects in this book can be sewn by hand. Feel free to use any materials to embellish and add your own personal touches. By creating festive decorations, you will have lots of fun not only on Christmas Day but days and weeks beforehand. Many projects are suitable for gifts, too, so lots of smiles are on their way.

Happy sewing and Merry Christmas!

Materials & tools

Fabrics

Felt fabric

There are different kinds of felt sheets on the market: synthetic, synthetic and wool mix and pure wool. Pure wool is always nice and soft to the touch but it is not an absolute requirement for this book. However, choose fabric that is not loosely woven so that the seams don't easily come apart.

Polyester or cotton wadding/batting

This is usually used in quilting, and for the projects in this book, it gives volume to thin objects and is also used as stuffing. Cotton wadding/batting can be sewn in the same way as felt fabric to add character to dolls' clothes and animal skins.

Printed fabric

You only need a very small amount, so you can use up scraps from your fabric stash.

Viscose surgical tubular gauze, size 01

This is to shape the doll's head before it is covered with skin-colour cotton stockinette. Choose the lightweight type, 1.5cm (½in) wide, size 01. It is the smallest size, used for small toes and fingers in clinics.

Skin-colour cotton stockinette

This is two-way stretchy fabric, ideal for making dolls' faces and limbs. It is widely available from doll-making suppliers and natural toy shops. The stockinette comes in different thicknesses and weights. Choose thin, light stockinette because the dolls in the book are small and have delicate features.

Thread

You can use ordinary sewing or embroidery thread to sew felt. Strong upholstery thread is used to tie dolls' necks and create an eyeline dent. If you would like to make a discreet seam when you need to sew two different colours together, it is a good idea to use invisible thread. I have also used fingering (4-ply) and DK (8-ply) yarn for embroidery. Some ornaments are hung with pearl cotton embroidery threads, size 05. You can use any thread, yarn or cord.

Stuffing

Polyester toy stuffing is used for most of the projects. If you struggle to stuff small parts, dolls' shoes for example, use stuffing wool or cotton wool.

Other materials

To construct the bases, you will need heavy and lightweight card, masking tape and glue. Recycle boxes used for postage for heavyweight card. For the lightweight card, reuse cereal boxes. You will need artificial flower peps for stamens. These can be found in craft shops. Polystyrene balls are used to make baubles.

You can embellish your projects with ribbons, hemp cord, small bells, jump rings or beads if you like.

Tools

Pens to mark fabric

I use ballpoint pen for most fabric, but air erasable pen for white fabric and white charcoal pencil for black.

Tracing paper and pencil

For transferring the designs.

Sewing needles

I use ordinary sewing needles and a blunt darning needle, and a sharp-pointed chenille needle with a large eye to embroider eyes and noses and sew on hair.

Fabric, thread and paper scissors

Remember never to cut paper with your good fabric scissors as it will blunt them.

Rulers

You will need a metal ruler and a set square (which helps with the angles of the gingerbread house).

Rotary fabric cutter and cutting mat

These are not essential but will help you cut fabric precisely. For straight lines, you can save yourself the trouble of marking the fabric.

Sewing machine

All projects can be sewn by hand, but you can achieve a clean finish for larger animal projects if you use a sewing machine. If you are not too confident about sewing small gussets, hand sew the tricky parts and use the machine for the rest of the project. Alternatively, cut out templates without seam allowances and blanket stitch all round by hand.

Bamboo chopstick

This is an amazingly useful tool. Turn the fabric inside out aided by a chopstick, and you can push small parts right out to the edge. You can also use it to help you stuff dolls and animals.

Using the templates

For easier tracing and sewing, some templates have bold lines and dotted lines. Cut at the bold line and sew about 3mm (⅛in) inside the edge.

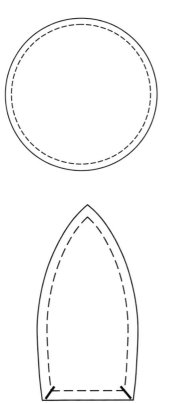

- A bold line is the cutting line, a dotted line is the sewing line.

- A red dotted line (see below) is the fold line.

- The two short bold digonal lines indicate an opening. If you start at bottom left, sew right round the shape to the line at bottom right, leaving an opening for stuffing. After stuffing, sew between these lines to close.

A seam allowance should be added where indicated. Mark your fabric using the template and cut 5mm (¼in) outside the line.

Tips

- Use household items such as thread cones, bobbins, ribbon reels etc. to mark circles.
- It is easier to cut straight lines using a rotary cutter and cutting mat.
- For small, intricate patterns, it is sometimes easier to cut freehand, without marking the fabric first.

Embroidery stitches

Back stitch

This is used to attach manes and to create hair and beards, some eyes, mouths and leaf veins.

1 Bring the needle up at A and pull the thread through. Insert the needle at B and bring it through at C. Pull the thread through the fabric.

2 Insert the needle at D and bring it up at E. Pull the thread through.

3 Insert the needle at F and bring it up at G. Continue working along the stitch line until it is completed. To finish off, thread your needle through the stitches on the wrong side of the work.

Blanket stitch

This is used to make feathered edges for wings and tails; to sew together hats and shoes, the Gingerbread House and the manger; to suggest the cut edges of biscuits; and to embroider blankets and other items.

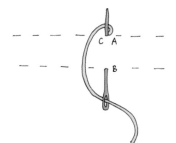 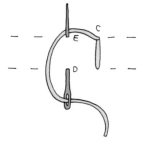 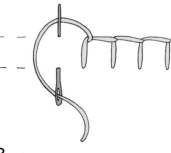

1 Bring the needle up at A and insert it at B to make a loop, then bring it through at C, inside the loop and right beside where you first came up. Pull the thread through.

2 Insert the needle at D, creating a loop, and bring it through at E, inside the loop.

3 Continue in this way.

French knot

These are used for eyes and noses. Take the needle through the yarn, separating the fibres, instead of taking the needle out between the stitches. This prevents the features from sinking into the face.

1 Bring the thread through where the knot is required at A. Holding the thread between your thumb and finger, wrap it round the needle twice.

2 Hold the thread firmly with your thumb and turn the needle back to A. Insert it as close to A as possible, at B, and pull the thread through to form a knot.

3 To hide the yarn end when you have finished making French knots for eyes and noses, take the needle out at the back of the head, then stitch into the head and trim the end.

Ladder stitch

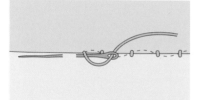

1 Hide your knot on the wrong side.

2 Pinch the edges of the fabric together. Make a small stitch on one side, then make another stitch on the other side. Keep your stitches running along the edge and pull the thread all the way through. Stitches will disappear into the two sides of the fabric.

Making the dolls

Basic doll and Yule log children

1 Work a gathering thread along one end of the tubular gauze and pull tightly. Turn inside out.

2 Stuff the tube. Tie a strong cotton thread 2cm (¾in) from the top. Upholstery thread is better than normal sewing thread.

3 Tie another thread halfway up the head to create the eyeline dent.

Tip

To tie a thread without losing tension, wrap the thread twice round the neck, thread one end underneath both wraps and pull firmly. This technique should be used to make the eyeline dent as well.

4 Stretch the stockinette over the head to make the face. The fabric grain should run vertically as shown. Tie the neck with skin-colour cotton thread. Gather excess fabric at the back of the head to avoid wrinkles under the chin. Draw tightly.

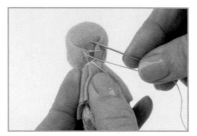

5 Thread the cotton thread used to tie the neck onto a needle and stitch excess fabric at the back of the head with overcast stitches, finishing with a French knot.

6 Use the basic doll body template on page 92 to make a red felt shape. Wrap around the doll, overlapping by 5mm (¼in) at the neck, and stitch the fabric at the neck.

Materials

Tubular gauze, size 01, 10cm (4in)

Toy stuffing

Skin-colour cotton stockinette, 7cm (2¾in) W x 8cm (3⅛in) L plus two pieces of 2 x 2cm (¾ x ¾in) for hands

Red felt, 18 x 18cm (7 x 7in)

Black felt, 6 x 6cm (2⅜ x 2⅜in)

White felt, 7 x 16cm (2¾ x 6¼in)

Strong cotton thread such as upholstery thread, white, skin-colour and red

Dark brown and brown fingering (4-ply) yarn and skin-colour DK (8-ply) yarn

Templates, page 92

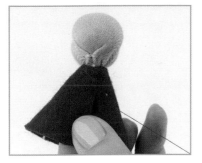

7 Overlap the join by 10mm (³/₈in), sew the back seam of the body with overcast stitches.

8 Work a gathering thread along the bottom edge.

9 Stuff and draw gently.

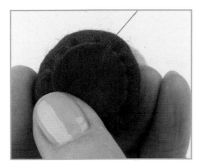

10 Make a felt base in red felt using the basic doll base template and stitch to attach with overcast stitches.

11 Use the templates rto make shoe pieces from black felt. Sew the side panel to the sole with blanket stitch.

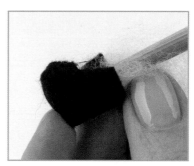

12 Sew the top of the shoe and stuff. Make two.

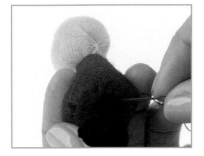

13 Sew the shoes to the base of the body.

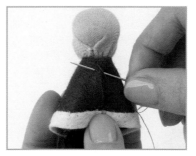

14 Use the template to make the coat in red felt and the coat trim in white felt. Sew the trim to the coat. Wrap round the body, overlapping a little and sew up the back seam.

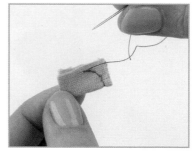

15 Fold the 2 x 2cm (¾ x ¾in) stockinette in half and stitch one end as shown to make the hand. Use skin-colour thread; red is used here for clarity.

15

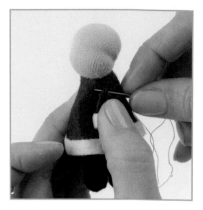

16 Turn the piece inside out and stitch the side seam with ladder stitch, folding the seam allowance inwards.

17 Make a red felt sleeve from the sleeve template and add a white trim from that template. Hold the hand in the centre of the sleeve end, fold the sleeve in half lengthwise and sew on the hand. Sew the sleeve seam.

18 Make a second arm and sew both arms onto the body.

19 With skin-colour DK (8-ply) yarn, French knot the nose. Take the needle in through the back of the head.

20 With dark brown fingering (4-ply) yarn, French knot the eyes. To hide the yarn end when finished, take the needle out at the back of the head, then stitch into the head and trim the end.

21 Make a red felt hat from the hat template and a white trim from the hat trim template. Place the trim on the hat with half protruding and sew on using white thread. Fold over the other side and sew to attach.

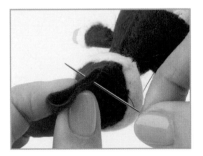

22 Attach to the head with white thread, through the trim, then blanket stitch the seam of the hat with red thread.

23 Make hair by sewing small back stitches with brown yarn, leaving large loops. For different styles, see Hansel and Gretel, page 68.

Shepherd doll

This doll is the basis for all the shepherds in The Christmas Story (page 78), as well as Joseph and the kings. Begin by making up the head and face as in steps 1 to 5 for the basic doll (page 14).

Materials

Tubular gauze, size 01, 10cm (4in)

Toy stuffing

Skin-colour cotton stockinette, 7cm (2¾in) W x 8cm (3⅛in) L plus 2 pieces of 2 x 2cm (¾ x ¾in) for hands

Yellow-green felt, 12 x 18cm (4¾ x 7in)

Brown felt, 13 x 16cm (5⅛ x 6¼in)

Strong cotton threads, white, skin-colour, yellow-green and brown

Templates, page 93

1 Make a shepherd body from yellow-green felt using the template on page 93. Fold in half and sew part-way up the seam as shown. Use back stitch if you are hand sewing.

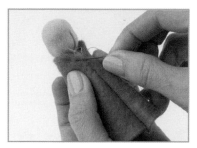

2 Turn inside out and place the head inside with the seam at the back. Sew up the remainder of the seam with ladder stitch in yellow-green thread. Sew round the neck in the same way to secure.

3 Stuff the body and run a gathering thread round the bottom. Make a base from the template and sew it on.

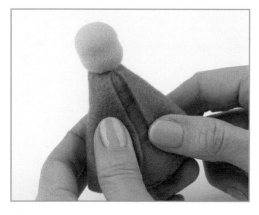

4 Use the template to make a coat in brown felt and stitch this on to the figure in a few places round the neck. The shepherd doll forms the basis for shepherd B (shown right) and also for shepherds A and C and other figures in The Christmas Story project. See individual instructions to finish.

Making animals

Donkey

This is how most of the animals are sewn. Start with the head gusset when the pattern has one and move on to the larger parts. If you are not using a sewing machine, use back stitch to give strength to the seams. Start by using the templates on page 94 to cut out all the felt pieces.

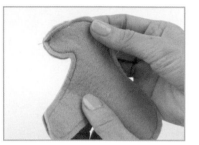

1 Place the two body pieces right sides together. Place the head gusset piece between the body pieces, matching points A, B and C. Sew the gusset in place from A to B to C on both sides.

2 Sew the top of the body and under the chin (C to D and A to E).

Materials

Grey felt, 25 x 25cm (10 x 10in)

White felt, 5 x 5cm (2 x 2in)

Strong cotton thread in grey

Brown fingering (4-ply) yarn

Lightweight card, 2 x 7cm (5 x 2¾in)

Toy stuffing

Templates, page 94

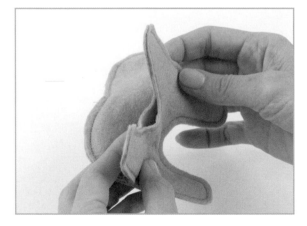

3 Sew on the tummy gusset, D to E, leaving an opening of 2–3cm (¾–1¼in) on one side for stuffing.

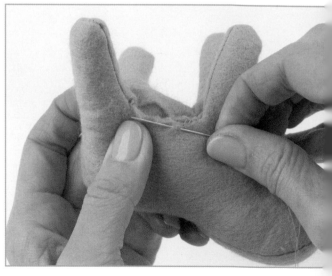

4 Turn right sides out and stuff the body firmly to the tips. Sew up the opening using ladder stitch to close the body.

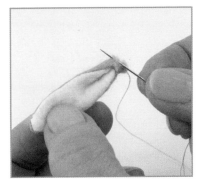

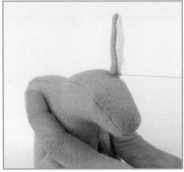

5 Sew the ears, each with one grey and one white side, and turn inside out. Fold the seam allowance at the base inwards and close the opening. Stitch the corners of the base together as shown.

6 Sew the ears to the head.

7 For the mane, wind brown fingering (4-ply) yarn round the card 100 times then sew a line along the centre, going over it twice to keep the yarn in place. Cut the loops and release the card. Attach the mane to the head with back stitch.

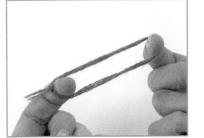

8 For the tail, cut brown fingering (4-ply) yarn to 80cm (31½in) and tie the ends together. Double the length three times. With a finger at each end, twist the length of yarn as shown. Place the tied end through the loop and tie the end. Cut the tied end of the loops and sew the other end to the body.

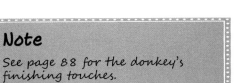

Note
See page 88 for the donkey's
finishing touches.

Christmas Tree Decorations

Embroidered baubles

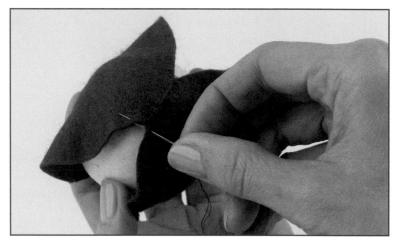

Materials

To make one bauble:

6cm (2³⁄₈in) polystyrene ball

Red felt, 10 x 18cm (4 x 7in)

Beige felt, 23 x 5cm (9 x 2in)

Yellow-green felt, 5 x 20cm (2 x 8in)

Yellow felt, 5 x 5cm (2 x 2in)

Strong cotton thread in red, beige, yellow-green and yellow and embroidery threads in colours of your choice

Toy stuffing

Scrap of lightweight card for top bobble

Scraps of felt in colours of your choice for motifs

Fabric glue

Gold string

Templates, page 95

1 Using the templates on page 95, cut out the top and bottom circles in red felt to cover the polystyrene ball. Sandwich the ball with the two circles and sew the edges together in one place to secure, taking the needle over and under about 2mm (¹⁄₈in). Leave the thread attached. Starting from the opposite side, sew half the ball, pulling and stretching the fabric as you encase the ball. It is a tight fit. Repeat on the other side. Do not worry about wrinkles or small gaps showing through, as this part will be hidden by the centre band.

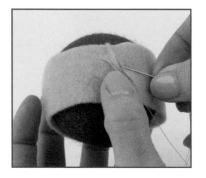

2 Use the template to make the centre band in beige felt and wrap it round the ball, stitching together the bias-cut ends with beige thread. Sew the edges to the bauble with overcast stitches.

3 Use the templates to make the top and bottom strips in yellow-green felt and sew them over and under the centre band with overcast stitches. Start from the edge touching the centre band, then the far edge. Cut the excess strip and stitch the ends together.

4 For the top bobble, cut the piece from yellow felt. Work a gathering thread in yellow along the edge of the circle and stuff with a little toy stuffing. Place the card circle on top and draw the thread tightly. Attach to the top of the bauble.

5 Use the templates to cut out felt from the scraps for the motifs, attach to the bauble with fabric glue and a few small stitches round the edge. Embroider as shown in the templates. Attach a hanging loop using the gold string.

Christmas pudding

1 Use the templates on page 96 to cut out all the felt pieces. Place the dark brown bottom felt circle on the polystyrene ball and work a brown gathering thread along the top edge, connecting the dots in the template. Draw tightly.

2 Place the dark brown top circle felt and sew to the edge of the bottom circle, as for the embroidered baubles on page 22.

3 Sew the cream piece of felt to the top with cream overcast stitches.

4 Work a red gathering thread along the red berry felt circle, stuff the berry and draw tightly.

Materials

5cm (2in) polystyrene ball

Dark brown felt for bottom and top circles

Cream felt, 9 x 9cm (3½ x 3½in)

Red felt scraps for holly berries

Green felt, 4 x 6cm (1⅝ x 2⅜in) for holly leaves

Strong cotton thread in brown, red and cream

Toy stuffing

Gold string

Templates, page 96

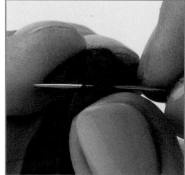

5 Work a second gathering thread outside the previous stitches and pull tight to shape the berry. Repeat steps 4 and 5 to make a second berry.

6 Sew on two holly leaves at the centre of the cream and attach the berries.

7 Attach a hanging loop using the gold string.

Gingerbread man

1 Cut two outline body shapes from brown felt using the template on page 96. Use the same template to cut cotton wadding/batting if using.

2 Sandwich the wadding/batting and sew all round the edges with blanket stitch. Alternatively, sew round the body and lightly stuff with toy stuffing.

3 Cut all the decorative pieces and glue them to the body.

4 Attach a hanging loop using red string.

Christmas stockings

Stocking with gifts

1 Use the templates on page 97 to cut two stockings in red felt and sew them together with blanket stitch. Leave the top open.

2 Use the top band template to make a white felt trim and sew the bottom edge to the stocking using overcast stitches. Fold the top edge inwards and sew from inside to outside to secure the band.

 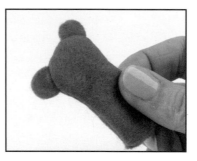

3 Use the teddy template to cut two pieces in brown felt. With the right sides together, sandwich the ears with the round side facing down and secure them, stitching outside the sewing line as shown.

4 Sew round the edges of the body, leaving the bottom open. Turn inside out, stuff, and close the seam.

5 Cut out the muzzle in beige felt and stitch to the face with overcast stitches. French knot eyes and nose with dark brown yarn. Make the scarf with pink felt and tie it on.

6 Cut two candy cane pieces from white felt. Sew them together, leaving an opening. Turn inside out, stuff and close the seam. Wrap with red felt strips and secure with overcast stitches.

7 Fold the the gift box felt piece in half lengthwise and sew together with overcast stitches. Flatten with the seam in the centre. Fold as shown (right) and secure with stitches. Tie the box with red string and make a bow in the centre. Stitch the bow with cotton thread. Place all the gifts in the stocking, securing them with a few stitches if needed and add a hanging loop using green string or yarn.

Materials

For stocking: red felt, 14 x 7cm (5½ x 2¾in); white felt, 2 x 12.5cm (¾ x 5in)

For teddy: brown felt, 7 x 6cm (2¾ x 2⅜in); beige felt, 2 x 2cm (¾ x ¾in); pink felt, 7cm x 0.8cm (2¾ x ⅜in)

For candy: white felt, 10 x 4cm (4 x 1⅝in); red felt, 20 x 0.8cm (8 x ⅜in)

For gift box: yellow-green felt, 5 x 9cm (2 x 3½in)

Strong cotton thread in red, white, brown, beige and yellow-green

Toy stuffing

Red and green string or yarn

Dark brown yarn for eyes and nose

Templates, pages 97

Stocking with puppy

1 Make the stocking as shown opposite. Use the templates on page 98 to make the puppy pieces in cream felt. For the head, work running stitch round the edge of the circle, stuff and draw tightly. Make stitches on alternate sides of the base with ladder stitch and pull the thread tightly to make an oval shape.

2 Sew up the body's side seam with back stitch, turn inside out and stuff. Work a gathering thread along the bottom and sew on the base with overcast stitches. Attach the head.

Materials

Cream felt, 16 x 7cm (6¼ x 2¾in)

Brown felt, 3.5 x 2cm (1³⁄₈ x ¾in)

Red felt, 7.5 x 3cm (3 x 1⅛in)

White felt, 7.5 x 2cm (3 x ¾in)

Toy stuffing and small amount of fleecy white yarn

Strong cotton thread in cream, white, red and brown

Dark brown yarn for eyes, nose and mouth

Green string or yarn

Templates, pages 98

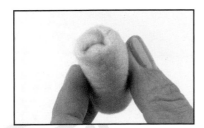

3 To make a paw, fold the square piece of cream felt in half horizontally and stitch the corner as in the basic doll's hand, step 15, page 15. Turn inside out and sew the rest of the seam with ladder stitch. Fold in the ends and attach to the body. Repeat for a second paw.

4 Make the hat from red felt, sew the seam and turn inside out. Sew the white edge to the hat, sandwiching the red fabric. Attach the hat to the head. With dark brown yarn, French knot the eyes and embroider the mouth and nose with back stitches. Cut two ears from brown felt, fold in half vertically, stitch the base corners together and attach over the hat. Add a scarf from fleecy white yarn. Place in the stocking and attach a hanging loop using green string or yarn.

Dove

Materials

White felt, 20 x 20cm (8 x 8in)

Small amounts of red and yellow felt

Strong cotton thread in white, yellow and red

Dark brown fingering (4-ply) yarn

Toy stuffing

String or yarn

Templates, page 98

1 Make the pieces from white felt using the templates on page 98. Sew the body seam, leaving the tail end open. Turn inside out and stuff.

2 Blanket stitch round the edges of the tail pieces, leaving a gap. Stuff lightly, then close the gap. With a threaded needle, pierce through the tail end to make the indented pattern. Insert the tail in the open tail end of the body and secure with overcast stitches.

3 Make the beak piece from yellow felt and wrap this round the tip of the head. Attach with stitches. With dark brown fingering (4-ply) yarn, French knot the eyes.

4 Make the wings the same way as the tail. Attach to the body.

5 Make the ribbon from red felt, tie a bow and stitch it to the neck.

6 Attach a hanging loop using string or yarn.

Angel

1 Make the head and body as for the basic doll on page 14. Make the body piece from white felt using the template on page 99, wrap it round the neck and sew the back seam. There is no base circle to sew on for this project. Leave the bottom edge open.

2 Make the skirt piece in white felt. Sew the side seam and turn inside out. Work a gathering thread along the top edge, insert the body and secure the skirt to the body with a few stitches.

3 Stuff lightly and sew the front and back edges of the hem together with blanket stitch. Wrap a white felt belt round the body, tie it at the back and secure with a few stitches. Cut any excess.

4 Make the hands and sleeves (in white felt) as for the basic doll, shown in steps 15–18 on pages 15–16. Sew on the arms.

5 Wind honey-yellow yarn round the card 15 times and take the card out. Secure the yarn on the top and sides of the head with a few stitches.

6 With skin-colour yarn, French knot the nose. With dark brown yarn, French knot the eyes. Attach metallic gold thread cord or ribbon to the head for the halo.

7 Use the templates to make organza wings. Work a gathering thread in the centre lengthwise and attach to the back of the body. Attach a hanging loop.

Tip
Wet the wing edges with a little glue to prevent fraying.

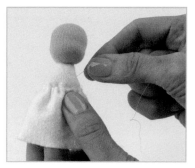

Materials

Tubular gauze, size 01, 10cm (4in)

Skin-colour cotton stockinette, 7cm (2¾in) W x 8cm (3⅛in) L plus two pieces of 2 x 2cm (¾ x ¾in) for hands

White felt, 8 x 20cm (3⅛ x 8in)

White silk organza fabric, 10 x 10cm (4 x 4in)

Strong cotton thread in white

Toy stuffing

Small amounts of dark brown and honey-yellow fingering (4-ply) yarn and skin-colour DK (8-ply) yarn

Card, 4 x 15cm (1⅝ x 6in)

8cm (3⅛in) metallic gold thread cord for jewellery making or gold ribbon

String or yarn and fabric glue

Templates, page 99

Toy soldiers

Begin by following the basic doll instructions steps 1 to 5 on page 14 to make the head and body.

1 Use the template on page 100 to make the trouser piece in white felt. Fold in half and sew down from the top edge diagonally and then straight down to the hem, following the sewing line on the template. Arrange so that the seam is in the centre. Sew the inside leg and crotch, again following the template.

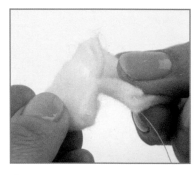

2 Cut up to the crotch to create the two legs.

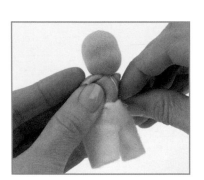

3 Turn inside out and sew to the body.

4 Make the shoe pieces from black felt. Follow the method for the basic doll on page 15, steps 11–12, to make each shoe. Stuff the legs and insert the tops of the shoes. Secure them with a few stitches.

Materials

To make one:

Tubular gauze size 1, 11cm (4³/₈in)

Skin-colour cotton stockinette, 7cm (2¾in) W x 8cm (3¹/₈in) L plus two pieces of 2 x 2cm (¾ x ¾in) for hands

White felt, 9 x 3cm (3½ x 1¹/₈in)

Red/green felt, 4 x 7.5cm (1⁵/₈ x 3in); 2 pieces 2.5 x 2.5cm (1 x 1in)

Yellow felt, 3 x 1.5cm (1¹/₈ x ⁵/₈in)

Black felt, 5 x 7cm (2 x 2¾in)

Dark brown felt, 5 x 11cm (2 x 4³/₈in)

Cream felt, 0.4 x 4cm (¹/₈ x 1⁵/₈in) for green soldier

Strong cotton thread in white, red, yellow, black and dark brown

Small amounts of dark brown fingering (4-ply) yarn and fair skin-colour DK (8-ply) yarn

Toy stuffing

Fabric glue

Gold string or yarn

Templates, page 100

5 Make the jacket in red felt, wrap it round and sew the seam at the back. Make the belt from dark brown felt and attach it with a few stitches around the waist and along the seam at the back.

6 Make the hands and sleeves (in red felt) as for the basic doll, shown on pages 15–16. Make the epaulettes in yellow felt and stitch the base edges to the sleeves. Attach the arms to the body.

7 Make the hat pieces from dark brown felt. Make a tube from the hat side, sew the seam and turn inside out. Attach the top with blanket stitches all round. Insert the head and secure with stitches.

8 With fair skin-colour yarn, French knot the nose. Use dark brown yarn to French knot the eyes. With dark brown yarn, attach a chin strap to the sides of the head. Glue on white buttons or strips.

9 Attach a hanging loop using gold string.

Snowman

Materials

White felt, 15 x 8cm (6 x 3$\frac{1}{8}$in)

Dark brown felt, 14 x 5cm (5½ x 2in)

Orange felt, 1.5 x 1cm ($\frac{5}{8}$ x $\frac{3}{8}$in)

Yellow-green felt, 1.5 x 15cm ($\frac{5}{8}$ x 6in)

Strong cotton thread in white, dark brown, yellow-green and orange

Toy stuffing

Fabric glue

Green string

Templates, page 101

1 Use the templates on page 101 to cut out two body pieces and the base in white felt. Sew the seam, leaving the bottom open. Turn inside out and stuff. Work a gathering thread along the bottom of the body and pull gently. Attach the base with overcast stitches.

2 Make arms from white felt. To make one arm, fold the square piece in half horizontally and stitch the corner, as in the basic doll's hand, step15, page 15. Turn inside out and sew the rest of the seam with ladder stitch. Repeat for the second arm. Fold in the ends and attach each arm to the body.

3 Make the hat pieces from dark brown felt. Make the hat side piece into a tube, sew up the seam and turn inside out. Attach the top circle with blanket stitches. Place the brim over the head, place the rest of the hat and secure with a few stitches.

4 Make the carrot nose form orange felt, fold it in half at the folding line and sew the side seam from the tip. Attach the base of the cone to the face without stuffing.

5 With dark brown yarn, French knot the eyes.

6 Make the buttons from dark brown felt and glue them to the body.

7 Make the scarf from yellow-green felt, tie it round the neck and secure it to the body with a few stitches.

8 Attach a hanging loop using green string.

Teddy bear

Materials

Brown felt, 20 x 20cm (8 x 8in)

Strong cotton thread in brown

Toy stuffing

Dark brown fingering
    (4-ply) yarn

15cm (6in) ribbon

Red string

Templates, page 101

1 Make all the teddy pieces from brown felt, using the templates on page 101.

2 Sew the head gusset to the two head panels, matching points A and B as for the donkey (page 18). Sew the rest of the head seam, leaving the neck edge open. Turn inside out, stuff and close the opening with ladder stitch.

3 Sew the two body pieces together, leaving an opening as shown. Turn inside out, stuff and close the opening. Repeat for the arms and legs.

4 Attach the limbs to the body as shown.

5 Make the four ear pieces and sew them together in twos, leaving an opening at the bottom. Turn inside out, stuff, fold the bottom seam allowance inside and close the opening. Fold each ear in half lengthwise and stitch the bottom corners together. Sew to the head.

6 With dark brown fingering (4-ply) yarn, French knot the eyes and embroider the nose and mouth with back stitches.

7 Tie the ribbon in a bow round the neck as shown and attach a hanging loop using red string.

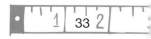

Robin

1 Use the templates on page 99 to make two bottom of body pieces in off-white felt and two top of body pieces in dark brown felt. With right sides facing, sew the top and bottom pieces together at the centre line. Open up so the new single piece is flat. Repeat for the other side. With right sides facing, sew two sides together from A (on the template) right round the edge to B, leaving the gap as shown. Turn inside out. Stuff and close the opening with ladder stitches.

2 Make two tummy pieces in red felt. Sew them together where marked, turn right sides out and attach to the body with overcast stitches.

3 Make four wing pieces from brown felt. Sew them together in twos by blanket stitching round the edges and attach them to the body as shown.

4 Make the beak from yellow felt, fold it in half and attach the edge to the body.

5 French knot the eyes with black fingering (4-ply) yarn.

6 Attach a hanging loop using green string.

Materials

Off-white felt, 12 x 6cm (4¾ x 2³⁄₈in)

Dark brown felt, 6 x 6cm (2³⁄₈ x 2³⁄₈in)

Red felt, 6 x 4cm (2³⁄₈ x 1⁵⁄₈in)

Brown felt, 5 x 6cm (2 x 2³⁄₈in)

Yellow felt, 1.5 x 1.5cm (⁵⁄₈ x ⁵⁄₈in)

Strong cotton thread in off-white, dark brown, brown, red and yellow

Toy stuffing

Black fingering (4-ply) yarn

Green string

Templates, page 99

Pink rabbit

Materials

Pink felt, 6 x 12cm (2³⁄₈ x 4¾in)

Dark pink felt, 4 x 4cm (1⁵⁄₈ x 1⁵⁄₈in)

Strong cotton thread in pink

Toy stuffing

Dark brown fingering (4-ply) yarn

12cm (4¾in) ribbon

Pink string

Templates, page 100

1 Use the templates on page 100 to make all the pieces from pink felt. Sew two body pieces together, leaving the base open. Turn inside out and stuff. Fold in the bottom seam allowance and stitch to close with ladder stitch.

2 Make two more ear pieces from dark pink felt. Sew each pale pink piece to a dark pink piece, leaving the bottom open. Turn inside out and stuff. Fold the bottom seam allowance inside and ladder stitch to close.

3 Fold each ear lengthwise and stitch the base corners together. Attach the ears to the head. French knot the eyes with dark brown fingering (4-ply) yarn.

4 Tie the ribbon in a bow round the neck and secure with a few stitches.

5 Make a tail circle from dark pink felt. Work a gathering thread round the edge and draw tightly. Attach to the body.

6 Attach a hanging loop using pink string.

Penguin

Materials

White felt, 6 x 8cm (2³⁄₈ x 3¹⁄₈in)

Black felt, 8 x 8cm (3¹⁄₈ x 3¹⁄₈in)

Red felt, 10 x 4cm (4 x 1⁵⁄₈in)

Yellow felt, 2 x 2cm (¾ x ¾in)

Strong cotton thread in white, black, red and yellow

Toy stuffing

Patterned fabric or ribbon, 3 x 20cm (1¹⁄₈ x 8in)

Dark brown fingering (4-ply) yarn

1cm (³⁄₈in) gold bell

Green string

Fabric glue

Templates, page 102

1 Use the templates on page 102 to make the front and back body pieces in black and white felt respectively. Make the head front piece in black felt and glue it to the white body piece.

2 With right sides facing, sew the body together, leaving the bottom edge open. Turn inside out and stuff the body. Close the opening.

3 Cut the beak from yellow felt. Attach it to the face as shown, sewing the middle horizontally.

4 Make four wing pieces from black felt. Place them together in twos and blanket stitch round the edges. Sew onto the body.

5 With dark brown fingering (4-ply) yarn, French knot the eyes.

6 Make the hat piece from red felt. Make it into a tube, sew the seam and turn inside out. Blanket stitch round the edge. Attach a gold bell at the tip.

7 Place the hat on the head and turn up the brim. Attach with a few stitches.

8 Fold the patterned fabric or ribbon in three lengthwise and tie it round the neck as a scarf.

9 Attach a hanging loop using green string.

Woodland fairies

Poinsettia fairy

1 Use the template on page 103 to cut out the body pieces in green felt. Sew the two body pieces together with blanket stitches, leaving the top and wrists open. Make hands as for the basic doll, steps 15 and 16, pages 15–16, and secure them to the wrists with a few stitches. Stuff the body lightly.

2 Make the head following steps 1–5 for the basic doll on page 14. Insert the stockinette in the neck gap of the body and secure it with stitches.

3 Use the templates to cut out large and small poinsettia petals from red felt. Embroider them as shown with back stitches in dark brown yarn or embroidery thread.

4 Fold artificial flower peps in half and sew the folds to the neck as shown below. Attach two large petals to the front and three to the back. Attach three small petals to the front and two to the back.

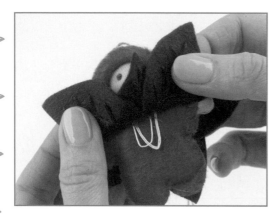

5 Make the hat from green felt, form a cone shape and sew the seam. Attach it to the head with the seam at the back. Fold back the brim.

6 With fair skin-colour yarn, French knot the nose. With dark brown yarn, French knot the eyes.

7 Attach a hanging loop using green string.

Materials

To make both fairies:

Green felt, 10 x 10cm (4 x 4in)

Red felt, 15 x 15cm (6 x 6in)

Yellow-green felt, 5 x 10cm (2 x 4in)

Tubular gauze, size 01, 10cm (4in)

Skin-colour cotton stockinette, 2 pieces of 7cm (2¾in) W x 8cm (3⅛in) L plus four pieces of 2 x 2cm (¾ x ¾in) for hands

Small amounts of fair skin-colour DK (8-ply)

Small amounts of yellow-green and dark brown fingering (4-ply) yarn or embroidery threads

Toy stuffing

Strong threads in green, red and yellow-green

3 double-ended artificial flower peps as stamens (available from craft shops)

Green string

Templates, page 103

Holly fairy

1 Make as for the poinsettia fairy, with the body in yellow-green felt and the hat in red.

2 Make two holly leaves using the template on page 103 in green felt and embroider them as shown with yellow-green yarn or embroidery thread.

3 Attach the leaves at the neck. Make two holly berries in red felt, as for the Christmas pudding on page 24. Attach the berries over the holly leaves as shown.

Santa Claus

Santa

Materials

Tubular gauze, size 01, 13cm (5$^1/_8$in)

Skin-colour cotton stockinette, 8 x 8cm (3$^1/_8$ x 3$^1/_8$in) plus two pieces of 2 x 2cm (¾ x ¾in) for hands

Red felt, 15 x 15cm (6 x 6in)

White felt, 4 x 8cm (1$^5/_8$ x 3$^1/_8$in)

Dark brown felt, 4 x 10.5cm (1$^5/_8$ x 4$^1/_8$in)

Strong cotton thread in red, white and dark brown

Toy stuffing

Small amounts of yellow, dark brown and fair skin-colour fingering (4-ply) yarn

Templates, page 104

1 Follow the basic doll instructions steps 1 to 5 on page 14 to make the basic head and body.

2 Use the template on page 104 to make Santa's body in red felt. Sew up the seam, leaving the top and bottom open. Turn inside out.

3 Insert the stockinette body and secure the red felt body at the neck, making small stitches all round. Work a gathering thread along the bottom edge and stuff.

4 Make the base from red felt and attach with overcast stitches.

5 Make the sleeves from red felt and the cuffs from white felt, then follow steps 15–18 from the basic doll on pages 15–16 to make the hands and sleeves and attach to the body.

6 Make the belt from dark brown felt and attach it to the body. Embroider the buckle with back stitches in yellow yarn.

7 Cut two shoe circles from dark brown felt. Run a gathering thread around the edge, stuff and draw tightly. Attach to the body.

8 Cut the hat from red felt, sew up the seam and turn inside out. Make a hat trim band from white felt, sandwich the edge of the hat and sew on.

9 With fair skin-colour fingering (4-ply) yarn, French knot the nose. With dark brown yarn, French knot the eyes.

10 Attach a little toy stuffing to the chin with cotton thread.

Sleigh

Materials

Burgundy felt, 16 x 24cm (6¼ x 9½in)

Cream felt, 12 x 12cm (4¾ x 4¾in)

Heavyweight card, 12 x 12cm (4¾ x 4¾in)

Strong cotton thread in burgundy, cream and white

Off-white cotton fabric, 11 x 11cm (4⅜ x 4⅜in)

Small amount of brown fingering (4-ply) yarn

A4/legal size card and oddments of Christmas wrapping paper, ribbons

Templates, page 105

1 Use the template on page 105 to cut out the sleigh twice in burgundy felt and once in strong heavyweight card. Sew round it, leaving the base open. Turn inside out. Insert the heavyweight card sleigh.

2 Close the bottom with ladder stitch.

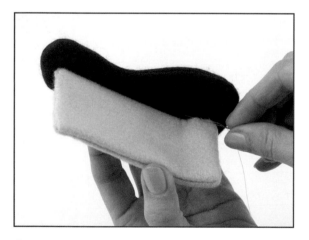

The finished sleigh.

3 Cut out two base panels in cream felt and in heavyweight card. Sew round the edge, leaving the back edge open. Turn inside out. Insert the heavyweight card and close the back seam.

4 Bend the back of the base panel upwards 1cm (³/₈in) from the rear end and sew the side panels onto the base panel.

Santa's sack

5 Cut out the sack in cotton fabric. Sew the side seam and place this in the centre. Sew the bottom seam. Fold in the top twice and stitch the edge with overcast stitches.

6 Turn right sides out. Loosely tie brown fingering (4-ply) yarn a third of the way down the bag.

7 Make up boxes with card using templates on page 122 and wrap them with wrapping paper. Tie ribbons and place them in Santa's sack.

Reindeer

Materials

To make one:

Dark brown felt, 23 x 23cm (9 x 9in)

Khaki felt, 10 x 16cm (4 x 6¼in)

White felt, 1 x 1cm (³/₈ x ³/₈in)

Yellow felt, 2 x 6cm (¾ x 2³/₈in)

Red felt, 1 x 5cm (³/₈ x 2in) and 0.5 x 12cm (¼ x 4¾in)

Strong cotton thread in dark brown, khaki, red and yellow

Toy stuffing

Small amount of golden yellow embroidery thread

Small amounts of dark brown, brown and red (for Rudolf) DK (8-ply) yarn

6mm (¼in) gold jingle bell and 2 x 5mm (¼in) jump rings

2 red 50cm (19¾in) strings to connect animals if you are making the whole set

Templates, page 106

1 Use the templates on page 106 to cut out two bodies in dark brown felt. Sew the chest, head and back seam (A to B). There is no head gusset.

2 Cut out the tummy gusset piece in dark brown felt. Open out the legs of the body piece and place over the tummy gusset piece, matching points A and B. Sew round, leaving one side of the tummy open. Turn the piece inside out. Stuff and close the tummy.

3 Cut four antlers in khaki felt. Place them together in twos, sew round them, leaving the base open and turn inside out. Stuff and close the opening.

4 Cut two ears in dark brown felt. Fold each one in half vertically, stitch the base corners together and attach the ears to the head.

5 Make two tail pieces, one in dark brown, one in white felt and sew them together, leaving the base open. Turn inside out, fold in the base seam allowance and close the opening with ladder stitch. Fold in half lengthwise with the white on the inner side and stitch the base corners together. Attach the tail to the body with the white side up.

6 Use the outer rectangle of the blanket template to make a yellow piece and the inner one to make a red piece. Place red on top of yellow and embroider using golden yellow embroidery thread. Attach the blanket to the body using blanket stitches in yellow embroidery thread.

7 Attach the antlers. With dark brown yarn, French knot the eyes. With brown, French knot the nose. Use red for Rudolf of course!

8 Make the neck band in red felt and stitch to the body, crossing at the front. Attach a bell as shown.

9 Attach a jump ring to the centre base edge of the blanket on either side.

10 Wrap the leader's neck with the red string once, and thread through the jump rings to harness all the animals. Tie the end of the string and attach it to Santa's hand. Repeat for the other set.

Yule Log

Materials

Display stand:

Cake board, 30cm (11¾in) in diameter, 1cm (³/₈in) thick

Cream felt, 70 x 40cm (27½ x 15¾in)

Chocolate log and decorations:

Lightweight card for main log cake: 15 x 20cm (6 x 8in), 15 x 8cm (6 x 3¹/₈in), two pieces of 10 x 9cm (4 x 3½in)

Lightweight card for tree stump, two pieces of 7 x 7cm (2¾ x 2¾in), 19 x 3cm (7½ x 1¹/₈in)

Masking tape

Dark brown felt, 15 x 27cm (6 x 10⁵/₈in), 15 x 42cm (6 x 16½in), 18 x 3cm (7¹/₈ x 1¹/₈in), 23 x 3.5cm (9 x 1³/₈in)

Brown felt, 20 x 20cm (8 x 8in); light brown felt, 12 x 12cm (4¾ x 4¾in); off-white felt, 12 x 12cm (4¾ x 4¾in); green felt, 8 x 5cm (3¹/₈ x 2in); red felt, 7 x 10cm (2¾ x 4in); raspberry pink felt, 10 x 10cm (4 x 4in); navy blue felt, 5 x 10cm (2 x 4in); cream felt, 10 x 10cm (4 x 4in)

Cotton thread to match all felt colours

Toy stuffing

Cotton wadding/batting, 4 x 8cm (1⁵/₈ x 3¼in)

Transparent thread, 0.5cm (¼in) width gold ribbon about 15cm (6in), cocktail stick, brown pastel or face powder

Card, 3 x 3cm (1¹/₈ x 1¹/₈in)

Templates, pages 107 and 108 (log), 103 and 109 (decorations)

Note

Use this display stand for the Yule log and the gingerbread house on page 54.

Display stand

1 For top felt piece, place the cake board on the cream felt and cut a circle with a 2.5cm (1in) allowance all round. For the bottom, cut a circle 0.5cm (¼in) inside the cake board size.

2 Work a gathering thread along the edge of the top piece, encase the cake board and draw tightly.

3 Sew the bottom to the top piece at the edge, using overcast stitches.

Chocolate log

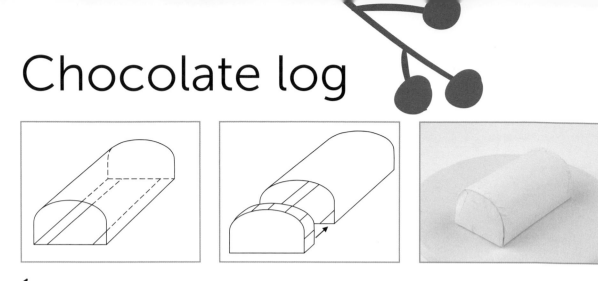

1 Construct the card log using the templates on page 107 and 108. Score along the fold lines with a knitting needle. Fold both ends of the top panel and attach it to the base panel with the sticking tabs folded inwards. Insert the sticking tabs of the end panels into the main body and secure them with masking tape.

2 Use the 15 x 27cm (6 x 10⅝in) piece of dark brown felt to cover the log and stitch the fabric together at the centre of the base with overcast stitches.

3 Cut felt panel end pieces from brown felt using the template on page 108. Make two cream motifs from light brown felt using the template on page 109 and attach to the end pieces with overcast stitches. Sew the end pieces to the log with overcast stitches.

4 Cut the 15 x 42cm (6 x 16½in) rectangle from dark brown felt for the second layer of the log. Wrap round the log and tack/baste together at the centre of the base.

5 Work a gathering thread around the end of the second layer as shown, stitching the fabric to the log from time to time to create texture.

6 Repeat at the other end of the log, then at intervals in between the two ends until the whole log is textured and the second layer is attached. Sew the base centre over the tacking/basting with brown thread, using small overcast stitches. Remove the tacking/basting.

7 Construct the card tree stump by cutting a 19 x 3cm (7½ x 1⅛in) card side panel and use the template on page 108 to cut the top. There is no base panel – the base is open. Use the dark brown 18 x 3cm (7⅛ x 1⅛in) felt piece for the side panel. Cut a brown felt top using the felt tree stump template on page 108. Use the template on page 109 to cut a cream motif in light brown felt and sew on to the felt top. Attach the felt top and side panels as for the log. Sew on the larger 23 x 3.5cm (9 x 1⅜in) dark brown felt side panel piece at the side edges with overcast stitches and texture it as for the log. Work a gathering stitch along the bottom edge and draw tightly. Sew the stump to the log.

The Yule log. See following pages for how to make the decorations.

Decorations

Raspberries and blueberries

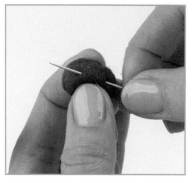

1 Use the templates on page 109 to cut raspberry pieces from raspberry pink felt and blueberry pieces from navy blue. For the raspberry, work a gathering thread around the felt circle, stuff and draw tightly to close. With invisible or dark pink cotton thread, indent lines by going over and across the body, pulling tightly and piercing through the centre each time.

2 Sew across each section with horizontal back stitches to create the bumps in the raspberry.

3 For the blueberry, work a gathering thread round the felt circle, stuff and draw tightly. Pierce the berry from the bottom to top a few times to create a dent in the centre. Attach to the log.

Mushrooms

1 Use the templates on page 103 to make the mushroom pieces from off-white felt. For the cap, work a gathering thread round the edge, stuff and draw the thread to shape. Attach the base of the cap with overcast stitches.

2 For the stalk, fold in half to make a cone shape, sew the side seam from the pointed tip and turn inside out. Work a gathering thread round the bottom edge, stuff and draw gently. Attach the base circle with overcast stitches. Attach the stalk to the base of cap.

Holly and berries

1 Use the template on page 109 to make two holly leaves in green felt. Stitch them together as shown. Make two red berry pieces and fold them in half. Stitch the round parts, leaving the base open. Turn inside out, stuff lightly and sew up the base. Attach to the centre of the leaves.

2 Sew the holly leaves to the cocktail stick and tie a gold ribbon to the stick. Insert the stick in the log.

Apple slices

1 Cut apple slices in cream felt using the templates on page 109. Cut four pieces of wadding/batting using the same template. Cut skin pieces in red felt. For each slice, layer a slice piece, wadding/batting then second slice piece. Attach the skin along the rounded edge with blanket stitch in invisible thread.

2 Attach all the slices together and place on the log. Stitch to the log if you wish.

Chocolate stars

1 Make the two sizes of star in brown felt and the smaller star in card, using the templates on page 109. Place the card star on the bottom star, then the top star. Sew some of the way round the edges.

2 Stuff and finish, sewing round the edges to close.

Children
The children are all variations on the basic doll shown on pages 14–16.

Gingerbread House

♥ House

Materials

House:

Heavyweight card, 30 x 45cm (11¾ x 17¾in)

Masking tape

Thin cotton fabric or calico, 14 x 16cm
(5½ x 6¼in), 3 x 48cm (1⅛ x 19in), 10 x 47cm
(4 x 18½in) (optional)

Liquid glue

Felt: beige, two pieces of 30 x 30cm (11¾ x
11¾in); brown, 20.5 x 25cm (8⅛ x 10in) for
roof; green to cover the inside (optional), 10 x
12.5cm (4 x 5in) and 41.5 x 8cm (16⅜ x 3⅛in)

Cotton wadding/batting, 26 x 21cm (10¼ x 8¼in)

Strong cotton thread in all the felt colours

Templates, pages 110–113

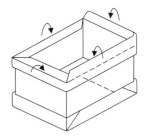

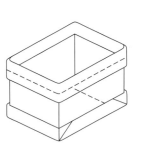

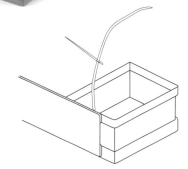

1 Use the templates for the house
(page 110), roof (page 111) and
chimney (page 113) to construct the
house in heavyweight card.

2 Stick on the thin cotton fabric
pieces for the base and half the
strip to cover the house using
liquid glue.

3 Make small cuts at the corners
of the top edge, fold down the
flaps and stick inside the box.
Insert the green lining felt (if used)
and glue it in place.

4 Now use the remainder of the
thin cotton strip. Fold down the
top and bottom edges, wrap it
round the house and sew it on to
secure.

The house, showing the thin cotton fabric being stitched in place.

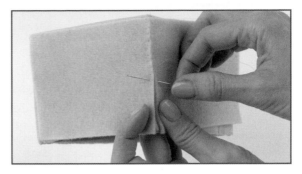

5 Cut beige felt panels for the sides of the house, two 8 x 13cm (3¹/₈ x 5¹/₈in) and two 8 x 10cm (3¹/₈ x 4in). Sew them in place with blanket stitch in matching thread as shown.

6 Place the wadding/batting on the roof and stitch it in place. Cover the roof and wadding/batting with the 20.5cm x 25 (8¹/₈ x 10in) brown felt piece. Fold in the edges and four corners and sew in place.

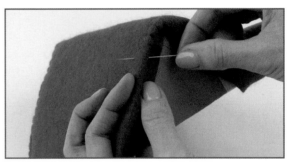

7 Starting from the apex of the gable end, insert the threaded needle from below, take it out on top and repeat. Stitch the edge, encasing 1cm (³/₈in) of the padded edge. Pull the thread fairy tightly to create indentations.

8 Use the template on page 112 to cut out the roof side panels in beige felt and sew on.

9 Make a cross-shaped incision in the felt roof over the chimney hole. Cut four beige felt panels 5 x 3.5cm (2 x 1³/₈in) to cover the chimney sides and one for the top 3.5 x 3.5cm (1³/₈ x 1³/₈in). Secure them with blanket stitch. Insert the chimney in the hole in the roof. You can secure it with a few stitches if desired.

Biscuits, cookies and decorations

Roof cream

1 Use the template on page 112 to cut eight pieces of white felt. Layer them and sew them together at the centre, using overcast stitches. Red thread is used in the photograph for clarity; use white.

2 Open out at the front to reveal the pattern. Make 16 and secure on the roof with stitches, as shown.

Materials

White felt, 3 x 16cm
(1⅛ x 6¼in)

Strong cotton thread in white

Template, page 112

Chimney cream

1 Cut four strips from the white felt, each 1 x 25cm (³⁄₈ x 10in). Layer them and sew them together in the centre as shown.

2 Coil the piece from one end, twisting and securing the piece with a few stitches to shape it. Attach to the chimney with stitches, as shown.

Materials

White felt, 5 x 26cm
(2 x 10¼in)

Strong cotton thread in white

Chimney chocolate

1 Use the template on page 112 to cut the circle from dark brown felt. Work a gathering thread round the edge, place toy stuffing in the centre and draw tightly.

2 Cut three thin strips of white felt, 3cm (1⅛in) long and glue them on the chocolate.

Chocolate door

1 Use the template on page 112 to cut panels A, B and C from heavyweight card. Glue A and B onto C as shown.

2 Cut two dark brown felt pieces, the top felt 4.5 x 6.5cm (1¾ x 2½in) and the bottom felt 4 x 6cm (1⅝ x 2⅜in). With blanket stitches, sew the felt panels together, sandwiching the heavyweight card in between.

3 With a threaded needle, stitch through the door at the bottom of panel A and the top of panel B, shown in red on the template.

Materials

Dark brown felt, 6 x 6cm (2⅜ x 2⅜in)

Strong cotton thread in dark brown

Small amount of white felt

Toy stuffing and glue

Template, page 112

Materials

Dark brown felt, 11 x 11cm (4⅜ x 4⅜in)

Heavyweight card, 6 x 6cm (2⅜ x 2⅜in)

Glue

Strong cotton thread in dark brown

Template, page 112

The coloured biscuits around the door are made from scraps of felt, using the templates on page 112. Cut two of each, sandwich a little toy stuffing in between and sew round the edges.

59

Basic biscuit: malted milk

Materials

Beige felt, 9 x 9cm (3½ x 3½in)

Heavyweight card, 3.3 x 4.3cm (1⅜ x 1¾in)

Strong cotton thread in beige

Brown pastel or brown face powder

1 Cut two rectangles from beige felt, one 4 x 5cm (1⅝ x 2in) and one 3.5 x 4.5cm (1⅜ x 1¾in). Sandwich the heavyweight card in between them. Sew all round the edge with blanket stitch.

2 Make indentations round the edge in the same way as for the roof (step 8, page 57).

3 To make the dots, pierce through the biscuit with a needle threaded with beige cotton thread and make French knots.

4 Brush the edge with brown pastel or brown face powder applied with a tissue.

Bourbon

Materials

Chocolate felt, 18 x 18cm (7 x 7in)

Dark brown felt, 3 x 5cm (1⅛ x 2in)

Heavyweight card, 6 x 10cm (2⅜ x 4in)

Strong cotton thread in dark brown

1 Follow steps 1–2 for the malted milk above, but with chocolate felt, to make two biscuits.

2 Sandwich the dark brown felt piece (the chocolate filling) between the biscuits, and with a needle threaded with dark brown thread, pierce through the biscuits, making French knots on each side.

Biscuit with piping

Materials

Beige felt, 8 x 7cm (3^1/$_8$ x 2¾in)

Strong cotton thread in beige

Heavyweight card, 3.3 x 4.3cm (1^3/$_8$ x 1¾in)

Brown pastel or brown face powder

1 Cut two rectangles from beige felt, one 4 x 6.5cm (1^5/$_8$ x 2½in) and one 3.5 x 4.5cm (1^3/$_8$ x 1¾in). Sandwich the heavyweight card between them. Sew the sides, leaving the top and bottom edges unsewn.

2 Pinch the centre and gather the fabric. Sew to secure.

3 Sew the top and bottom edges. Brush round the edges with brown pastel or brown face powder applied with a tissue.

Pretzel

Materials

Brown felt, two pieces 5 x 4cm (2 x 1^5/$_8$in)

Strong cotton thread in brown

Toy stuffing

Template, page 115

1 Use the template on page 115 to cut out the two pretzel shapes in brown felt. Sew the inner edges together with blanket stitches.

2 Sew the outer edges with blanket stitches, inserting a small amount of stuffing from time to time.

Salty cracker

Materials

Beige felt, 5 x 10cm (2 x 4in)

Strong cotton thread in beige

Cotton wadding/batting, 5 x 5cm (2 x 2in)

Templates, page 114

1 Use the template on page 114 to cut out the pieces in beige felt and wadding/batting. Sandwich the wadding/batting between the felt and sew the edges together with blanket stitch.

2 Make indentations on the edge and dots from French knots as for the malted milk biscuit on page 60.

Cream sandwich

Materials

Beige felt, 10 x 10cm (4 x 4in)

Pink or dark brown felt, 4 x 4cm (1⅝ x 1⅝in)

Strong cotton thread in beige and pink or dark brown

Heavyweight card, 7 x 4cm (2¾ x 1⅝in)

Lightweight card, 3 x 3cm (1⅛ x 1⅛in)

Templates, page 114

1 Cut out top and bottom pieces of each biscuit layer in beige felt, using the templates on page 114. Cut a heavyweight card circle 1mm (⅛in) smaller all round than the bottom piece. Follow steps 1–2 for the malted milk biscuit (page 60). Make two.

2 Cut another card circle 1mm (⅛in) smaller all round than the bottom felt panel. Cut the pink or dark brown felt for the cream, using the cream sandwich top biscuit panel. Work a gathering thread along the edge, encase the card circle and draw tightly.

3 Sandwich the cream piece and with a threaded needle, pierce through the biscuits, making French knots on each side.

Jammie dodger

Materials

Beige felt, 5 x 9cm (2 x 3½in)

Red felt, 6 x 6cm (2⅜ x 2⅜in)

Heavyweight card, 4 x 4cm (1⅝ x 1⅝in)

Strong cotton thread in beige

Brown pastel or brown face powder

Templates, page 114

1 Use the templates on page 114 to cut out the top and bottom in beige felt and the jam/jelly in red. Cut a heavyweight card circle 1mm (⅛in) smaller than the bottom.

2 Work a gathering thread round the edge of the jam/jelly circle, place the heavyweight card inside and draw tightly.

3 With blanket stitches, sew the top and bottom pieces together, sandwiching the jam/jelly. Brush the edges with brown pastel or brown face powder.

Choco-vanilla wheel

Materials

Two pieces each of chocolate and beige felt, 0.5 x 25cm (¼ x 10in)

Invisible thread

Fabric glue

1 Glue the two chocolate strips together, then do the same with the two beige pieces. Glue the two colours together in one long strip.

2 Wet with glue on top of the layers and roll. Secure the end with a pin and leave to dry. Remove pin.

3 Sew to secure, threading through the piece a few times.

Digestive

Materials

Beige felt, 5 x 10cm (2 x 4in)

Heavyweight card, 5 x 5cm (2 x 2in)

Strong cotton thread in beige

Brown pastel or brown face powder

Templates, page 114

1 These can be made either plain or decorated. Use the tempates on page 114 to cut out the top and bottom pieces in beige felt. If decorating, fold the top piece of felt and slice off a tiny amount of fibre with scissors. Cut heavyweight card 1mm ($^1/_8$in) smaller than the smaller bottom template.

2 With blanket stitches, sew top and bottom together with the heavyweight card in between.

3 Brush with brown pastel or brown face powder.

Icebox cookie

Materials

Cream felt, 4 x 8cm (1$^5/_8$ x 3$^1/_8$in), 1 x 16cm
    ($^3/_8$ x 6$^1/_4$in) for the side strip

Brown felt, 2 x 4cm (¾ x 1$^5/_8$in)

Chocolate felt, 2 x 4cm (¾ x 1$^5/_8$in)

Cotton wadding/batting, 4 x 4cm (1$^5/_8$ x 1$^5/_8$in)

Strong cotton thread in cream and brown

Template, page 113

1 Cut squares of cream felt 4 x 4cm (1$^5/_8$ x 1$^5/_8$in) for the top and bottom and wadding/batting the same size. Use the template on page 113 to make brown and chocolate squares and sew them on to one cream square.

2 Sew this to the side strip with blanket stitches. Insert the wadding/batting and sew on the other cream square.

Choco-cream biscuit

Materials

Cream felt, 7 x 7cm (2¾ x 2¾in)

Brown felt, 6 x 6cm (2³⁄₈ x 2³⁄₈in)

Lightweight card, 5 x 5cm (2 x 2in)

Strong cotton thread in brown and cream

Templates, page 113

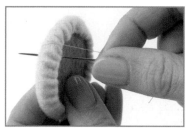

1 Using the templates on page 113, cut out the filling circle in brown felt and the biscuit circle in cream felt. Cut out the card circle. Work a gathering thread round the edge of the brown filling circle, encase the card and pull the thread tight. Work a gathering thread round the biscuit circle, encase the covered filling circle and pull tight. Pierce through the biscuit from the front inner edge and take the needle out from the back and repeat to make indentations all round the biscuit.

Little gems

Materials

To make one:

Beige felt, 3 x 6cm (1¹⁄₈ x 2³⁄₈in)

Pink, white, light blue or soft purple felt,
    4 x 4cm (1⁵⁄₈ x 1⁵⁄₈in)

Heavyweight card, 2 x 2cm (¾ x ¾in)

Lightweight card, 2 x 2cm (¾ x ¾in)

Strong cotton thread in matching colours

Templates, page 114

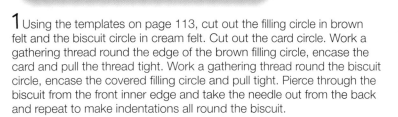

1 Use the templates on page 114 to make the beige felt top and bottom pieces and the lightweight card and heavyweight card pieces. With blanket stitches, sew the top and bottom pieces together with the heavyweight card circle sandwiched in the middle.

2 Make the cream piece from coloured felt. Thread a needle with matching thread and use it to connect the dots (from the template). Insert the lightweight card circle, draw tightly and make a knot.

3 Sew the cream to the biscuit.

Piped biscuit

Materials

Beige felt, 5 x 5cm (2 x 2in)

Small amount of dark brown felt

Lightweight card, 3 x 3cm (1⅛ x 1⅛in)

Strong cotton thread in beige

Toy stuffing

Fabric glue

Templates, page 115

1 Use the templates on page 115 to make the biscuit piece in beige felt and the card circle and chocolate piece in dark brown felt. Place the card circle in the centre of the beige felt piece and thread a needle to connect the dots, as in the little gems (see page 65).

2 Insert a little toy stuffing and draw tightly. Make a knot to finish.

3 Glue the chocolate to the centre.

Heart palmier

Materials

Two pieces of beige felt, 0.5 x 30cm (⅛ x 11¾in)

Brown felt, 0.5 x 13.5cm (⅛ x 5¼in)

Glue, clothes peg, hammer and clear seed beads

Strong cotton thread in beige

Brown pastel or brown face powder

1 Wet one side of one beige strip with glue and roll from the centre. Repeat for the other strip. Pinch the end with a clothes peg. Leave to dry.

2 Connect the two pieces at the centre with a few stitches.

3 Glue the brown strip to the outside and brush the surface with brown pastel or brown face powder.

4 Put clear beads in a bag, place on a suitable strong work surface and hit with a hammer. Wet the biscuit with glue where you want the sugar crystals, sprinkle on the broken beads and leave to dry.

Sugar-coated chocolate buttons

Materials

To make one:

Felt, colour of your choice, 3.5 x 3.5cm (1³/₈ x 1³/₈in)

Lightweight card, 1.5 x 1.5cm (⁵/₈ x ⁵/₈in)

Strong cotton thread to match

Templates, page 112

1 Use the templates on page 112 to make the felt and card pieces. Work a gathering thread round the felt, insert the card and draw tightly.

Cheese straw

Materials

Beige felt, 3 pieces 1 x 7cm (³/₈ x 2¾in)

Fabric glue

Strong cotton thread to match

Template, page 115

1 Use the template on page 115 to cut out three pieces in beige felt and glue them together. Twist the piece and sew the top and bottom edges to the corner of the house.

Flute

Materials

Beige felt, 7.5 x 7.5cm (3 x 3in)

Brown pastel or brown face powder

Fabric glue

Template, page 113

1 Use the template on page 113 to cut out the circle in beige felt. Brush the edge with brown pastel or brown face powder.

2 Wet one side of the edge with glue and roll up. Leave to dry.

Hansel & Gretel

Hansel

1 Make the head following steps 1–5 for the basic doll, page 14. Use the templates on page 116 to make shoes in white felt and attach these below the body, as in the basic doll steps 11–13 (see page 15).

2 Use the template to make the shirt from patterned fabric. Fold in 0.5cm (¹⁄₈in) of the neck edge and one of the side edges and attach to the body round the neck. Sew the seam at the back with overcast stitch. Fill the body with toy stuffing.

3 Use the template to make the overalls piece in light blue felt. Wrap the lower half of the body with it and stitch it together at the back. With a threaded needle, pierce through the crotch and go back and forth between the crotch and the hem to create legs.

4 Sew the arms and sleeves as for the basic doll, steps 15–18, pages 15–16, using the template on page 116. Since you are using fabric and not felt, fold in the edges of the sleeve piece before you sew the seams, to avoid fraying (see picture opposite step 5). Attach the arms.

5 To make straps, thread a length of light blue yarn and pierce the body from the top of the back of the trousers (on the left). Take the needle out at the right top corner of the chest piece. Place yarn over the shoulder, insert the needle back where you started and take it out at the left top corner of the chest pad. Place yarn over the shoulder, insert the needle to the top of the trousers on the right. Make a discreet knot.

6 Attach brown yarn hair, making back stitches on the sides of the face, leaving loops. With fair skin-colour yarn, French knot the nose. With dark brown, French knot the eyes.

7 Use the template to make the hat piece from brown felt. Work a gathering thread round the edge and draw gently. Insert head and secure it with a few stitches. Sew on the brim.

Gretel

1 Make the head and body following steps 1–5 for the basic doll, page 14.

2 Use the template on page 116 to make the shirt from patterned fabric. Fold in 0.5cm (⅛in) of the neck edge and one of the side edges and attach to the body round the neck. Sew the seam at the back.

3 Make the base from beige felt. Work a gathering thread along the bottom of the shirt and draw gently. Stuff the shirt and attach the base with overcast stitches.

4 Make the shoe and sole pieces in brown felt and make as in the basic doll steps 11 and 12 (page 15). Sew to the base of the body.

5 Sew the arms and sleeves as for the basic doll, steps 15–18, pages 15–16 using the arm template on page 116. Since you are using fabric and not felt, fold in the edges of the sleeve piece before you sew the seams, to avoid fraying (see below). Attach the arms.

6 Thread a length of brown yarn and pierce the head from the sides, leaving a long loop each time. Leave smaller loops at the forehead. Make plaits and tie the ends with red yarn. Make the headscarf piece in pink felt, sew the seam and attach to the head.

7 Make the apron from beige felt and attach it by sewing the seam at the back. Make straps with white yarn, piercing through the body as for Hansel opposite.

8 With fair skin-colour yarn, French knot the nose. With dark brown yarn, French knot the eyes.

Materials

Tubular gauze, size 01, 10cm (4in)

Skin-colour cotton stockinette, 7cm (2¾in) W x 8cm (3⅛in) L plus two pieces of 2.5 x 2.5cm (1 x 1in) for arms

Toy stuffing

Patterned cotton fabric, 10 x 5cm (4 x 2in)

Felt: beige, 5 x 10cm (2 x 4in); pink, 9 x 5cm (3½ x 2in); brown, 5 x 3cm (2 x 1⅛in)

Strong cotton threads to match felt and fabric

Small amounts of brown, dark brown, red and white fingering (4-ply) yarn and small amount of fair skin-colour DK (8-ply)

Templates, page 116

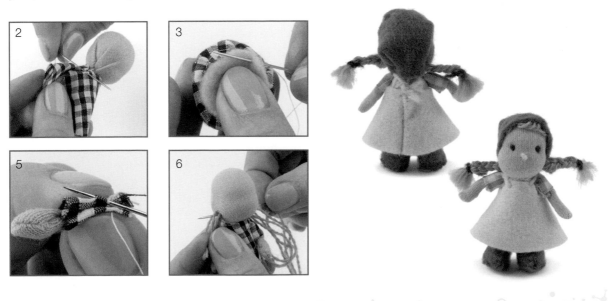

Fir tree

1 Use the templates on page 115 to cut two beige felt trees from part A and one yellow-green felt and one heavyweight card inner tree. Stitch the green tree on top of one of the beige ones.

2 With blanket stitches, sew the beige pieces together with the heavyweight card inner tree in between. Glue on white felt dots cut from the template.

3 Cut the soil top and base from brown felt. Make a small hole in the centre of the soil top using the tips of your scissors.

4 Work a gathering thread round the soil top and draw gently. Sandwich the heavyweight card circle between the base and top and using blanket stitches, sew two-thirds of the way round.

5 Fold the length of the garden wire in two and insert the folded end through the hole in the soil top. Bend the end about 1cm (^{3}/$_8$in) (see diagram below).

6 Stuff the soil piece and close the seam.

7 Insert the other end of the wire in the tree (see diagram).

Materials

Beige felt, 6 x 12cm (2^3/$_8$ x 4^3/$_4$in)

Yellow-green felt, 5 x 5cm (2 x 2in)

Brown felt, 6 x 4cm (2^3/$_8$ x 1^5/$_8$in)

White felt, 2 x 2cm (¾ x ¾in)

Strong cotton thread to match felt colours

Heavyweight card circle, 2cm (¾in) diameter, and piece 5 x 5cm (2 x 2in) for inner tree shape

Toy stuffing

Lightweight garden wire, 10cm (4in)

Fabric glue

Templates, page 115

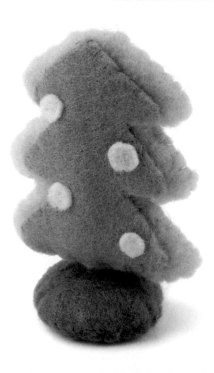

Holly Wreath

Pine cone

Materials

Brown felt, 5 x 25cm (2 x 10in)

Strong cotton thread in brown

Template, page 118

1 Use the template on page 118 to make a strip of brown felt (place the template on a fold to make the strip double the length of the template).

2 Roll the strip from one end to make a pine cone shape, securing it with a few stitches as you go.

Oak leaves and acorns

Materials

Yellow-green felt, 8 x 8cm (3⅛ x 3⅛in)

Khaki felt, 5 x 7cm (2 x 2¾in)

Brown felt, 8 x 8cm (3⅛ x 3⅛in)

Strong cotton thread in khaki and brown

Green embroidery thread

Fabric glue

Toy stuffing

Templates, page 117

1 Use the templates on page 117 to cut out the leaves in yellow-green felt. Embroider the leaves.

2 Cut out the acorn cap in khaki and the acorn in brown. Fold the acorn cap in half, sew the seam and turn inside out. Do the same with the acorn. Stuff the acorn and cap and connect them at the centre, using overcast stitches.

3 Cut out the stalk in khaki felt, wet one side with glue and roll from the edge. Leave to dry. Sew the stalk to the cap.

Rabbit

1 Use the templates on page 117 to cut out the pieces in white felt. Place the two body pieces together and blanket stitch all round, leaving the base open.

2 Stuff, fold in the base allowance and close the bottom of the body with ladder stitches.

3 Cut out the ear pieces and sew them onto the head.

4 With dark brown yarn, French knot the eyes.

Dove

1 Use the templates on page 117 to cut out the pieces in white felt. Sew the two body panels together with blanket stitches. Do not stitch the tail. Stuff the body and sew along the dotted line in the template, **piercing through both layers.**

2 Attach the wings with a few stitches. With dark brown yarn, French knot the eyes.

Fairy

Materials

Tubular gauze, size 01, 10cm (4in)

Skin-colour cotton stockinette, 7cm (2¾in)
W x 8cm (3⅛in) L plus two pieces of
2 x 3cm (¾ x 1⅛in) for legs

Toy stuffing

Light blue felt, 8 x 5cm (3⅛ x 2in)

White felt, 10 x 10cm (4 x 4in)

Light purple felt, 8 x 5cm (3⅛ x 2in)

Strong cotton thread in white, light blue
and light purple

Small amount of red and dark brown
fingering (4-ply) and fair skin-colour DK
(8-ply) yarn

Templates, pages 96 and 118

1 Make the head and body, following steps 1–10 on pages 14–15 for the basic doll, using the basic doll body template on page 96.

2 Make legs instead of arms, using the same method as for the basic doll's arms (steps 15–16, pages 15–16), but making the legs using the 2 x 3cm (¾ x 1⅛in) stockinette. Fold the ends inwards and attach to the body.

3 Use the template on page 118 to cut out the cape in light blue felt and attach it to the neck with stitches.

4 Cut out the wings in white felt. Blanket stitch round the edges. Attach them to the back.

5 With fair skin-colour yarn, French knot the nose. With dark brown, French knot the eyes.

6 Cut out the hat in light purple felt, sew the seam, turn inside out and attach it to the head. Fold the edge up to make a brim.

7 Make a bow with red yarn and sew it to the neck.

Bells

1 Use the templates on page 118 to cut out the bell twice, in yellow felt. Place together and sew the side seams, leaving the base open.

2 Cut out the card circle, using the template. Work a gathering thread along the base of the bell, insert the toy stuffing and place the card circle on top. Draw the thread tightly.

To finish

Make a bow with the ribbon (see page 72) and attach it to the top centre. Attach all the ornaments to the wreath, referring the photograph for guidance.

The Christmas Story

Mary

1 Make the head and body, following steps 1–10 for the basic doll on pages 14–15 but using the basic body and base templates on page 119 and salmon pink felt. Cut the cape from light blue felt and sew the centre point to the head.

2 Fold in the sides as shown. Take the needle down through the head and make a stitch under the chin.

3 Make the arms and sleeves following steps 15–18 for the basic doll, pages 15–16. French knot the nose with fair skin-colour yarn and the eyes with dark brown yarn.

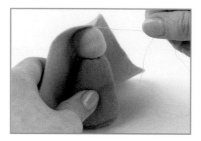

Joseph

1 Make up the head and body as for Mary, using the Shepherd body and base templates on page 93 and purple felt.

2 Cut out the coat from dark brown felt, using the template on page 120. Sew up the top of the hood with blanket stitch and turn inside out. Work a gathering thread to separate the hood from the coat. Pierce the doll through the neck to attach. Add arms and sleeves, as for Mary.

3 Thread a needle with grey bouclé yarn and sew on loops for the hair and beard.

4 French knot the nose with fair skin-coloured yarn and the eyes with dark brown yarn.

Materials

Mary:

Tubular gauze, size 01, 10cm (4in)

Skin-colour cotton stockinette, 7cm (2¾in) W x 8cm (3⅛in) L plus two pieces of 2 x 2cm (¾ x ¾in) for hands

Toy stuffing

Salmon pink felt, 8 x 15cm (3⅛ x 6in)

Light blue felt, 12 x 15cm (4¾ x 6in)

Strong cotton thread in light blue

Small amounts of fair skin-colour DK (8-ply) and dark brown fingering (4-ply) yarn

Joseph:

Stockinette, tubular gauze and toy stuffing as above

Purple felt, 8 x 15cm (3⅛ x 6in)

Dark brown felt, 11 x 15cm (4⅜ x 6in)

Strong cotton thread in dark brown

Small amounts of fair skin-colour DK (8-ply), dark brown fingering (4-ply) and grey bouclé yarn

Templates, pages 93, 119 and 120

Jesus

1 Make up the head as for the basic doll (steps 1–5, page 14) but make it smaller than the adult head by tying the stuffed tubular gauze 1.5cm (⁵⁄₈in) from the top. Embroider the eyes in back stitch using dark brown fingering (4-ply) yarn, then French knot the nose with skin-colour yarn.

Materials

Skin-colour cotton stockinette, 6cm (2³⁄₈in) W x 7cm (2¾in) L

Tubular gauze, size 01, 8cm (3¹⁄₈in)

White felt for blanket, 6.5 x 6.5cm (2½ x 2½in)

Brown felt, 13 x 12cm (5¹⁄₈ x 4¾in)

Strong cotton thread in white and brown

Card, 9 x 8cm (3½ x 3¹⁄₈in)

Liquid glue and toy stuffing

Small amounts of fair skin-colour DK (8-ply) yarn and dark brown fingering (4-ply) yarn

Templates, pages 120 and 121

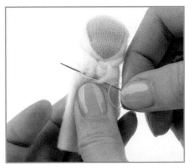

2 Use the template on page 120 to cut out the blanket in white felt. Place the head on the blanket and cover the baby's forehead with its top edge. Fold in the sides and stitch them at the neck.

3 Secure the front of the blanket with a few stitches as shown. French knot the nose with fair skin-colour yarn and embroider the eyes with dark brown yarn.

4 Make up the manger with card from the template on page 120. Cut out brown felt using the template on page 121 and place the card manger in the centre. Wet the inner card walls with liquid glue and fold in the felt flaps. Sew the outer side edges with blanket stitches.

5 Place the baby in the manger.

Shepherds

Shepherd A

1 Make up the shepherd doll following the instructions on page 17 and using the templates on page 93. Use light brown felt. Cut out the vest from wadding/batting using the template on page 123, and attach. Add arms following steps 15–18 for the basic doll, pages 15–16, using light brown felt.

2 Cut out the hat in dark brown felt from the template on page 123 and sew up the seam. Turn inside out, fold the tip of the hat inwards and attach to the head.

3 French knot the eyes with dark brown yarn and the nose with fair skin-colour. Tie the waist with brown yarn.

Shepherd B

1 Make up the shepherd doll, following the instructions on page 17 and the templates on pages 93 and 123. Use green felt. Add arms following steps 15–18 for the basic doll, pages 15–16, using brown felt and the template on page 123.

2 Use the template on page 123 to cut out the hat in cream felt. Work a gathering thread round the sewing line and attach it to head. Thread a length of brown yarn and work running stitch around the base of the hat. Make a bow at the end.

3 French knot the eyes with dark brown yarn and the nose with fair skin-colour. Make the hair and beard with grey bouclé yarn.

A

B

Materials

To make one shepherd:

Skin-colour cotton stockinette, 7cm (2¾in) W x 8cm (3⅛in) L plus two pieces of 2 x 2cm (¾ x ¾in) for hands

Tubular gauze, size 01, 10cm (4in)

Felt for body and base, 16 x 11cm (6¼ x 4⅜in)

Toy stuffing

Small amounts of fair skin-colour DK (8-ply) yarn and dark brown fingering (4-ply) yarn

Templates, pages 93 and 123

Add for shepherd A:

Light brown felt, 8 x 17cm (3⅛ x 6⅝in); dark brown felt, 5 x 8cm (2 x 3⅛in)

Cotton wadding/batting, 5 x 9cm (2 x 3½in)

Small amount of brown fingering (4-ply) yarn

Strong cotton thread in light brown and dark brown

Add for shepherd B:

Brown felt, 10 x 17cm (4 x 6¾in); cream felt, 6 x 6cm (2⅜ x 2⅜in)

Strong cotton thread in brown and cream

Small amount of brown fingering (4-ply) yarn and grey bouclé yarn

Add for shepherd C:

Khaki felt, 8 x 17cm (3⅛ x 6⅝in); grey felt, 15 x 5cm (6 x 2in); white felt, 7 x 5cm (2¾ x 2in)

Cotton wadding/batting 4 x 7cm (1⅝ x 2¾in)

Strong cotton thread in grey

Small amount of red-brown bouclé yarn

Shepherd C

1 Make up the shepherd doll, using steps 1–5, page 18 and the templates on pages 93 and 123. Use khaki felt.

2 Cut the vest from grey felt, using the template on page 123. Wrap round the body so the ends overlap by 3cm (1⅛in) and sew to secure at the back. Add arms following steps 15–18 for the basic doll, pages 15–16, using khaki felt.

3 Make hair with red-brown bouclé yarn. French knot eyes from dark brown yarn and the nose from fair skin-colour yarn.

4 Make the hat from the template on page 123. Fold in half, sew the seam and attach to the head.

5 Make the lamb following the instructions on page 88 and attach it to the body.

C

Kings

Red king

For the red king you will also need:

Red felt, 10 x 17cm (4 x 6¾in); purple felt, 4 x 4cm (1⁵⁄₈ x 1⁵⁄₈in); white felt, 1.5 x 7cm (⁵⁄₈ x 2¾in), dark pink felt, 1.5 x 4cm (⁵⁄₈ x 1⁵⁄₈in)

2 x 2cm (¾ x ¾in) gold wrapping paper, 3mm gold bead

Small amounts of gold and grey embroidery thread and light-brown bouclé yarn

1 Make up the red king following the shepherd doll instructions on page 17, up to step 3. Cut out the king's coat from red felt, using the template on page 124.

2 Embroider the coat with gold embroidery thread as shown. Attach the coat to the king's body at the neck. Embroider the sleeves. Add arms and red felt sleeves following steps 15–18, pages 15–16, for the basic doll. Attach to the king.

3 Use the template to cut out crown A in purple felt. Work a gathering thread round the edge and draw gently. Attach it to head.

4 Cut out the trim of the crown in white felt, fold in half and attach it to the crown.

5 With grey embroidery thread, make six lines across the top, piercing from the sides and crossing in the middle.

6 Attach a gold bead in the front centre of the crown. French knot the eyes with dark brown yarn and the nose with skin-colour yarn. With light brown bouclé, back stitch the hair and beard.

7 Make the cushion with the dark pink felt. Fold in half, sew round two edges, lightly stuff and sew to close. With gold thread, add fringes to the corners (see page 88, step 9 for the Camels). Roll the gold wrapping paper into a ball and stitch to the cushion. Stitch to the king's hands.

Blue king

For the blue king you will also need:

Blue felt, 10 x 17cm (4 x 6¾in); yellow felt, 3 x 7cm (1⅛ x 2¾in); light blue felt, 3 x 3cm (1⅛ x 1⅛in); yellow-green felt, 4.5 x 6.5cm (1¾ x 2½in)

2 x 2mm pearl beads, 1 x 3mm pink bead, 1 x 3mm gold bead

Small amounts of gold embroidery thread and grey bouclé yarn

Templates, pages 121 and 124

1 Make up the blue king following the shepherd doll instructions on page 17, up to step 3. Cut out the king's coat from blue felt, using the template on page 124. Embroider the coat as shown. Attach the coat to the king's body at the neck.

2 Embroider the sleeves. Add arms and blue felt sleeves following steps 15–18, pages 15–16 for the basic doll. Attach to the king.

3 With grey bouclé yarn, back stitch the hair and beard. French knot the nose with skin-colour yarn and the eyes with dark brown yarn.

4 Cut out crown B in yellow felt from the template on page 124. Attach the beads as shown and sew to the head with the seam at the back.

5 Use the templates on page 121 to cut out the gift 1 top in light blue felt and the gift 1 body in yellow-green felt. Work a gathering thread round the top piece, stuff and draw tightly. Sew the side seams only of the gift 1 body and turn inside out. Fold down the top as marked and stuff.

6 Work a gathering thread along the base edge and draw tightly to close. With a threaded needle, pierce the gift body from the base centre, take the needle out from the top and repeat. Pull the thread gently to flatten the base. Attach the top blue piece to the body of the gift. Attach a bead to the top and with gold thread, embroider the base of the top piece. Attach the gift to the blue king's hands.

Green king

> **For the green king you will also need:**
>
> Green felt, 10 x 17cm (4 x 6¾in); cream felt, 3 x 11cm (1⅛ x 4⅜in); yellow felt, 3 x 5cm (1⅛ x 2in); purple felt, 1 x 1cm (⅜ x ⅜in)
>
> Lightweight card, 3 x 5cm (1⅛ x 2in)
>
> 4mm blue bead, 6mm silver bead
>
> Small amounts of gold embroidery thread, red fingering (4-ply) yarn and dark brown bouclé yarn
>
> Templates, pages 121 and 124

1 Make up the green king as for the other two, using brown stockinette and green felt for the coat and sleeves.

2 With dark brown bouclé yarn, back stitch the beard.

3 Cut out the turban in cream felt using the template on page 124. Wrap it round the head from the back and stitch to secure.

4 Fold the edges in and sew to secure.

5 Fold the top down and ladder stitch to secure. Sew on a silver bead and a scrap of red yarn as shown.

6 Make up the gift 2 base with card, from the template on page 121, and wrap it with the yellow felt piece. Blanket stitch on all the side edges. Cut out the gift 2 top in purple felt and glue it on. Sew a blue bead on top. Attach the box to the green king's hands.

Animals

Sheep and lamb

Materials

For the sheep and lamb:

Fair skin-colour felt, 5 x 5cm (2 x 2in)

White felt, 3 x 3cm (1⅛ x 1⅛in)

Strong cotton thread in white and skin-colour

Toy stuffing

Small amounts of dark brown fingering (4-ply) yarn

Cotton wadding/batting, 16 x 15cm (6¼ x 6in)

Templates, page 125

Sheep

1 Cut out the pieces from the templates on page 125, all in white felt apart from the head and head gusset in skin-colour felt. Sew the two body pieces together. Sew the two tummy gusset pieces together, leaving the centre open. Sew the tummy gusset to the body. Turn the piece inside out. Stuff the body, but keep the tummy opening unsewn.

2 Sew the head gusset to the two head pieces. Sew from the nose to the chin and turn inside out.

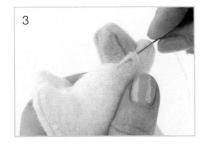

3 Insert the face in the opening of the body and sew them together, folding the face edge of the body inwards as you go. Stuff the face. Close the tummy opening.

4 Connect the base edges of the ears and attach to the head.

5 With threaded needle, pierce the base of the body back and forth to create legs.

6 With dark brown yarn, French knot the eyes.

Lamb

1 Cut out the body pieces in white felt and the head pieces in skin-colour felt, using the templates on page 125. Sew the body seam, leaving the head edge open. Turn inside out and stuff the body.

2 Sew the head pieces together, leaving the end that will join the body open. Turn inside out and stuff the head.

3 Insert the head in the body and sew in place. Attach ears as for the sheep.

4 French knot the eyes with dark brown yarn.

Donkey

Materials

As well as the materials needed for the basic donkey (see page 18) you will need:

Large brown blanket, 3 x 7.5cm ($1^{1}/_{8}$ x 3in)

Small beige blanket, 2 x 6.5cm (¾ x 2½in)

Yellow-green blanket, 4 x 8cm ($1^{5}/_{8}$ x $3^{1}/_{8}$in)

Small amount of brown fingering (4-ply) yarn

Dark brown embroidery thread

1 Make the basic donkey shown on pages 18–19 and stitch the eye using French knots. Place the smaller blanket on top of the larger one and blanket stitch all round both with dark brown embroidery thread. Attach the blanket to the donkey as shown.

2 Roll up the yellow-green felt blanket and tie it in two places with brown yarn. Attach it to the donkey as shown.

3 Attach the brown rope following steps A and B for the camels on page 91.

Ox

1 Cut the pieces using the templates on page 126, all in dark brown felt apart from the horns in skin-colour. Sew the head gusset to the two body pieces, matching points A and B to the head. Sew the back from B to C and under the chin from D to A.

2 Sew the two tummy gusset pieces together from D to E and F to C.

3 Sew the tummy gusset to the legs. Turn inside out and stuff. Close the opening.

4 Fold in and stitch the base corners of the ears and attach to the head.

5 Sew the horn pieces together leaving the base open. Turn inside out and attach them to head. There is no need to stuff them.

6 Cut light brown fingering (4-ply) yarn to 40cm (15¾in) and double the length three times. Cut dark brown felt to 1 x 3cm (³⁄₈ x 1¹⁄₈in) and place the yarn on top of the felt, with 1cm (³⁄₈in) of the yarn sticking out. Stitch the sides of the felt together, encasing the yarn. Cut the yarn loops and attach the tail to the body.

7 With a threaded needle, pierce the body base to create legs, as for the sheep, step 5 on page 87.

8 French knot the eyes with dark brown yarn.

Materials

Dark brown felt, 23 x 23cm (9 x 9in)

Skin-colour felt, 9 x 4cm (3½ x 1⁵⁄₈in)

Strong cotton thread in dark brown and skin-colour

Toy stuffing

Small amount of light brown fingering (4-ply) yarn

Small amount of dark brown DK (8-ply) yarn

Templates, page 126

Camels

Materials

To make one camel:

Beige felt, 20 x 30cm (8 x 11¾in); light blue/pink/yellow-green felt, 7 x 11cm (2¾ x 4³⁄₈in); cream/yellow-green/yellow felt, 3 x 7.5cm (1¹⁄₈ x 3in); brown felt, 2 x 2cm (¾ x ¾in); purple/red felt, 2 x 2.5cm (¾ x 1in); dark brown felt, 3 x 4cm (1¹⁄₈ x 1⁵⁄₈in); khaki felt, 3 x 8.5cm (1¹⁄₈ x 3³⁄₈in)

Toy stuffing

Strong cotton thread to match felt colours

Small amounts of embroidery thread

Small amounts of dark brown DK (8-ply) yarn and brown fingering (4-ply) yarn

Templates, pages 126–128

1 The seated and standing camels are made in the same way. Use the templates on page 127 for the seated camel and on page 128 for the standing one. Cut out the head gusset, tummy gusset and body pieces in beige felt. Sew the head gusset to the two body pieces.

2 Sew the top of the body from B to C. Sew the chest from D to A.

3 Sew the two tummy gusset pieces together, from point D to E and F to C. Sew the tummy gusset to the legs. Turn inside out, stuff and close the opening.

4 For the seated camel, with a threaded needle, pierce the base through the body back and forth to create legs, as for the sheep, step 5 on page 87.

5 Make a tail as for the Donkey, step 8 on page 19. Attach it to the body. Embroider the eyes with back stitch in dark brown yarn.

6 Use the template on page 127 to cut out the blanket. Embroider the edge with back stitches.

7 Make saddle ends as for the the ox's horns in brown felt (step 5, page 89; template page 126).

8 Cut out the smaller blanket and embroider with back stitches and French knots as shown.

9 Make fringes round both blankets as shown below. Loop a short length of embroidery thread through the eye of a needle as shown. Pull this through the blanket edge. Pull the ends through the loop.

10 Sew the larger blanket to the camel, then sew on the two saddle ends, one in front of and one behind the hump. Sew the smaller blanket on top as shown.

11 Cut out the outer and inner head ornament shapes from the templates on pages 127 and 128. Sew one on top of the other with overcast stitches. Attach the ornament to the head.

12 Cut out the bag in khaki felt from the template on page 127, fold in half, sew up the side seams and turn inside out. Tie the top with dark brown yarn.

13 Attach the brown yarn rope, following the steps A to E shown opposite.

A Insert the needle from right to left, through the camel's snout.

B Wrap the yarn round the snout, going under and over. Insert the needle from left to right and then from right to left again.

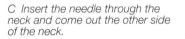

C Insert the needle through the neck and come out the other side of the neck.

D Wrap the yarn up over the head, then insert the needle back through the neck from left to right, in the same place as before.

E Stitch and secure the yarn at (a), then take the needle through the neck from right to left once more. Tie the ends.

Templates

All the templates are shown full size unless otherwise stated.

Basic doll, page 14 (and Yule log children)

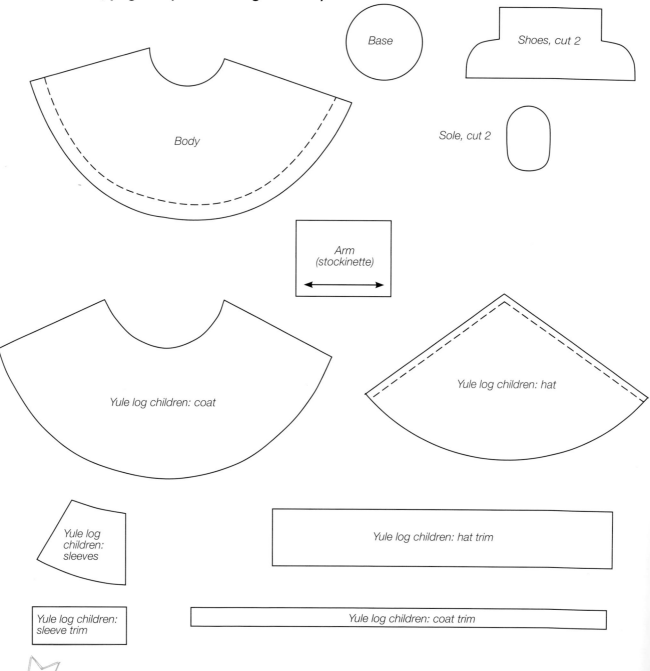

Base

Shoes, cut 2

Sole, cut 2

Body

Arm
(stockinette)

Yule log children: coat

Yule log children: hat

Yule log children:
sleeves

Yule log children: hat trim

Yule log children:
sleeve trim

Yule log children: coat trim

Shepherd doll, page 17

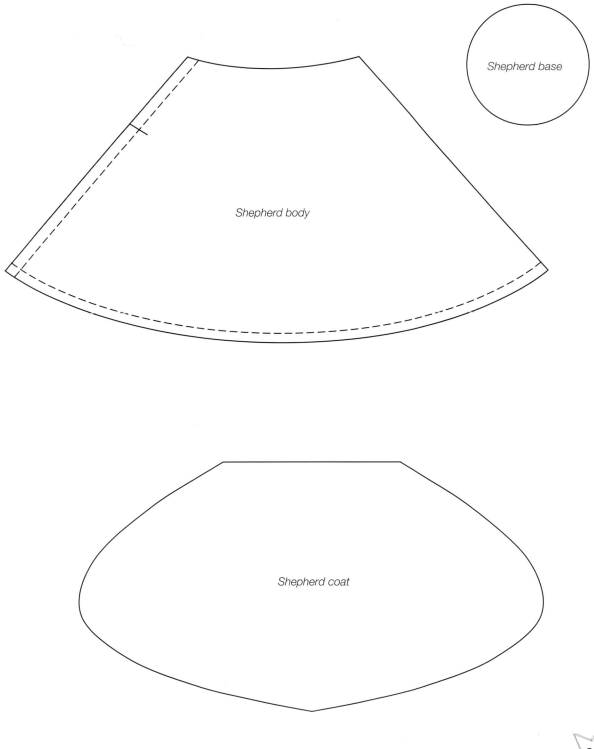

Shepherd base

Shepherd body

Shepherd coat

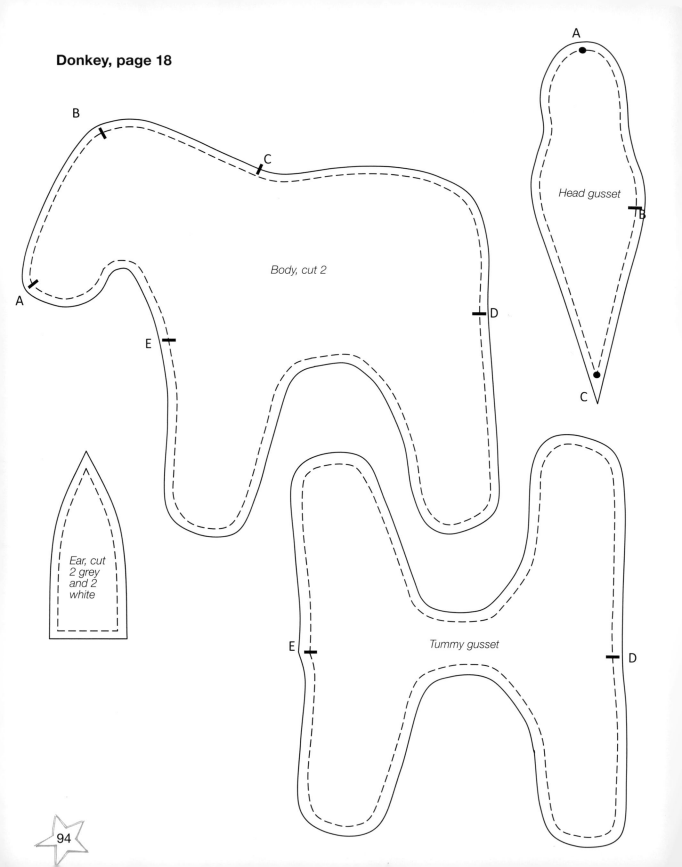

Donkey, page 18

B

C

A

Body, cut 2

E

D

A

Head gusset

B

C

E

*Ear, cut
2 grey
and 2
white*

D

Tummy gusset

Embroidered baubles, page 22

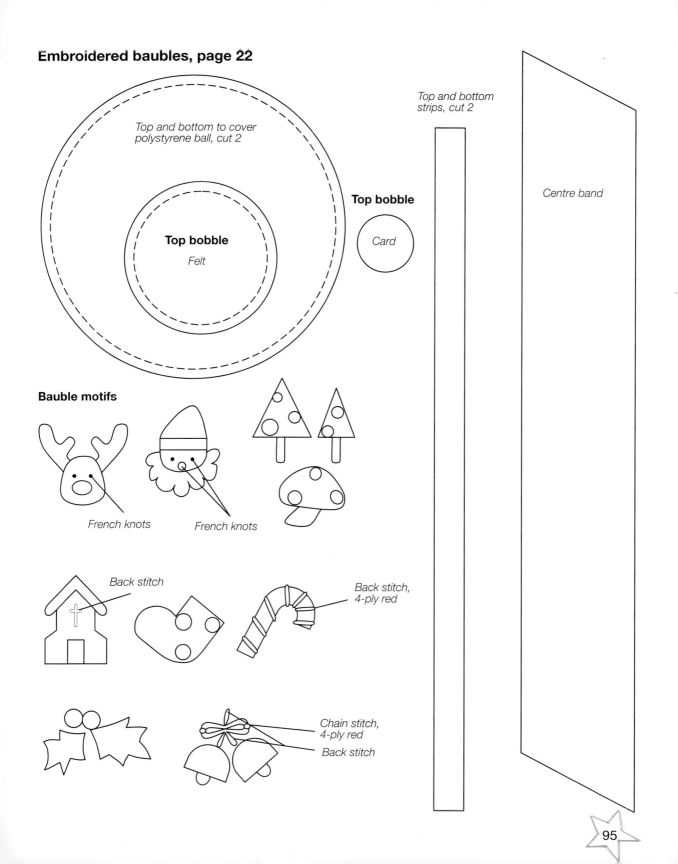

Top and bottom to cover polystyrene ball, cut 2

Top bobble
Felt

Top bobble

Card

Top and bottom strips, cut 2

Centre band

Bauble motifs

French knots

French knots

Back stitch

Back stitch, 4-ply red

Chain stitch, 4-ply red

Back stitch

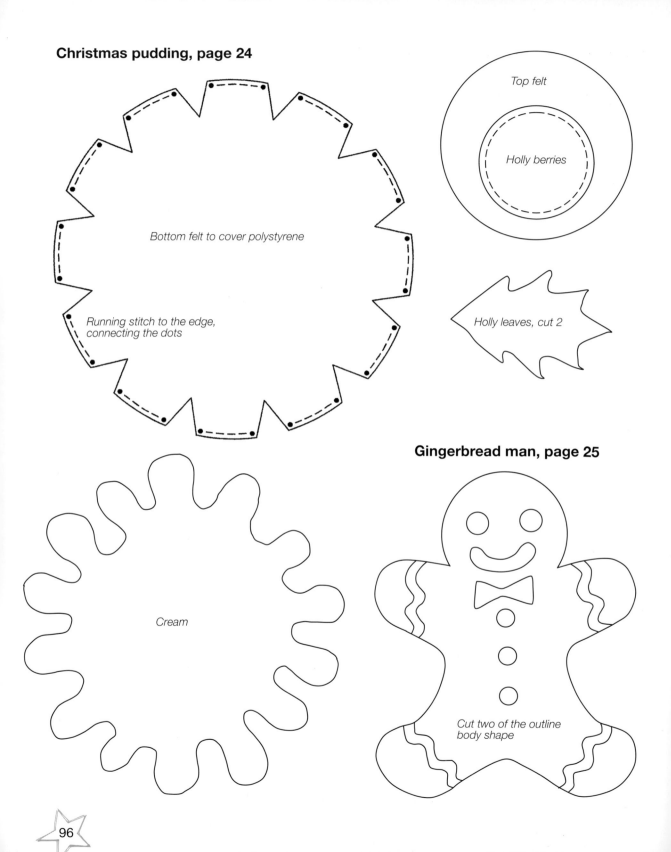

Christmas pudding, page 24

Top felt

Holly berries

Bottom felt to cover polystyrene

Holly leaves, cut 2

*Running stitch to the edge,
connecting the dots*

Cream

Gingerbread man, page 25

*Cut two of the outline
body shape*

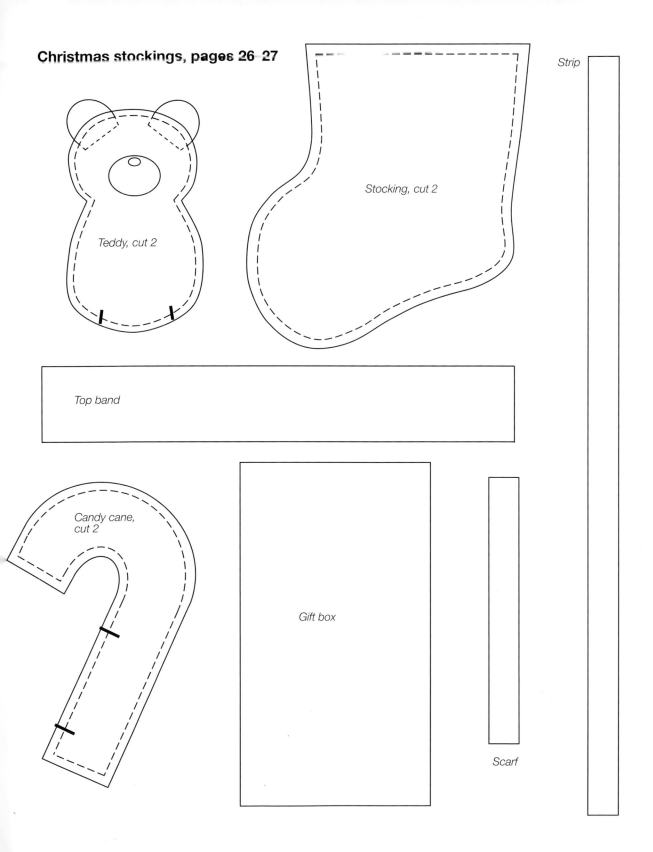

Christmas stockings, pages 26–27

Teddy, cut 2

Stocking, cut 2

Strip

Top band

Candy cane, cut 2

Gift box

Scarf

Christmas stockings continued

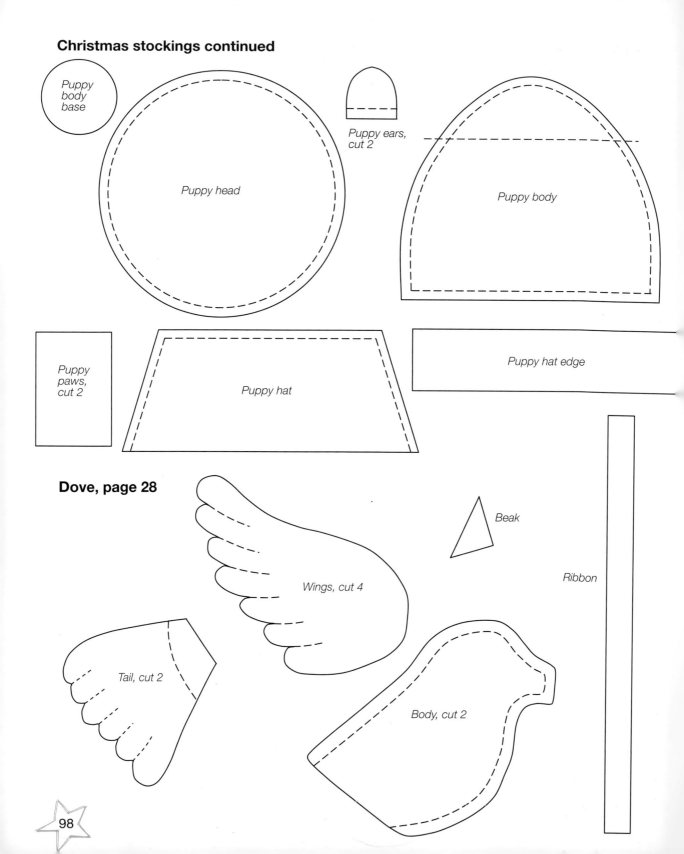

Puppy body base

Puppy head

Puppy ears, cut 2

Puppy body

Puppy paws, cut 2

Puppy hat

Puppy hat edge

Dove, page 28

Wings, cut 4

Beak

Ribbon

Tail, cut 2

Body, cut 2

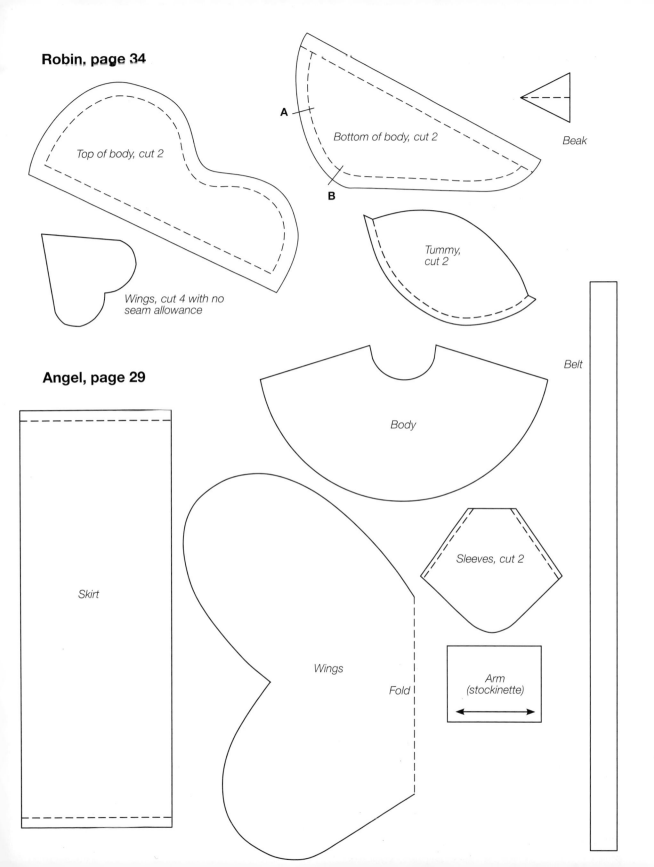

Robin, page 34

Top of body, cut 2

Bottom of body, cut 2

A

B

Beak

Wings, cut 4 with no seam allowance

Tummy, cut 2

Belt

Angel, page 29

Skirt

Body

Wings

Fold

Sleeves, cut 2

Arm (stockinette)

Toy soldier, page 30

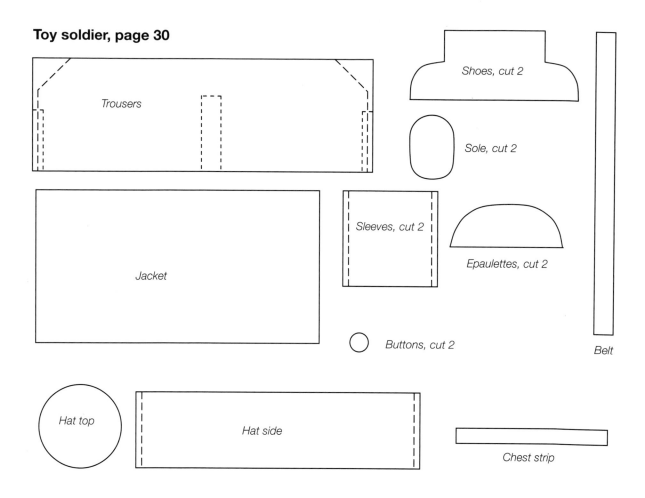

Trousers

Shoes, cut 2

Sole, cut 2

Jacket

Sleeves, cut 2

Epaulettes, cut 2

Buttons, cut 2

Belt

Hat top

Hat side

Chest strip

Pink rabbit, page 35

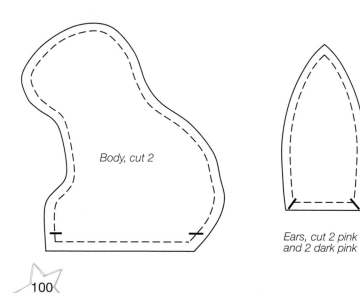

Body, cut 2

Ears, cut 2 pink
and 2 dark pink

Tail

Snowman, page 32

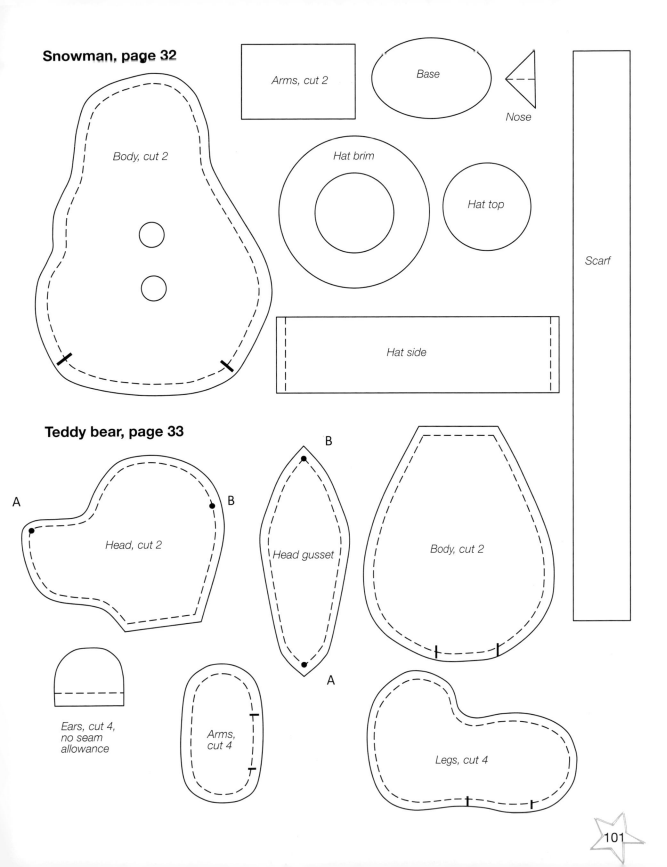

Arms, cut 2

Base

Nose

Body, cut 2

Hat brim

Hat top

Scarf

Hat side

Teddy bear, page 33

A

B

Head, cut 2

B

Head gusset

A

Body, cut 2

Ears, cut 4,
no seam
allowance

Arms,
cut 4

Legs, cut 4

101

Penguin, page 36

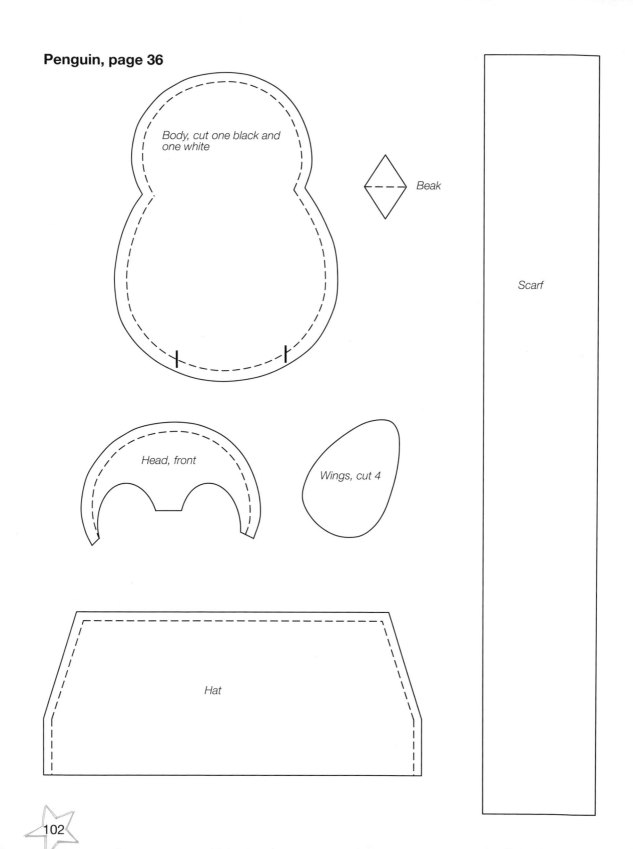

Body, cut one black and one white

Beak

Scarf

Head, front

Wings, cut 4

Hat

Woodland fairies, page 38

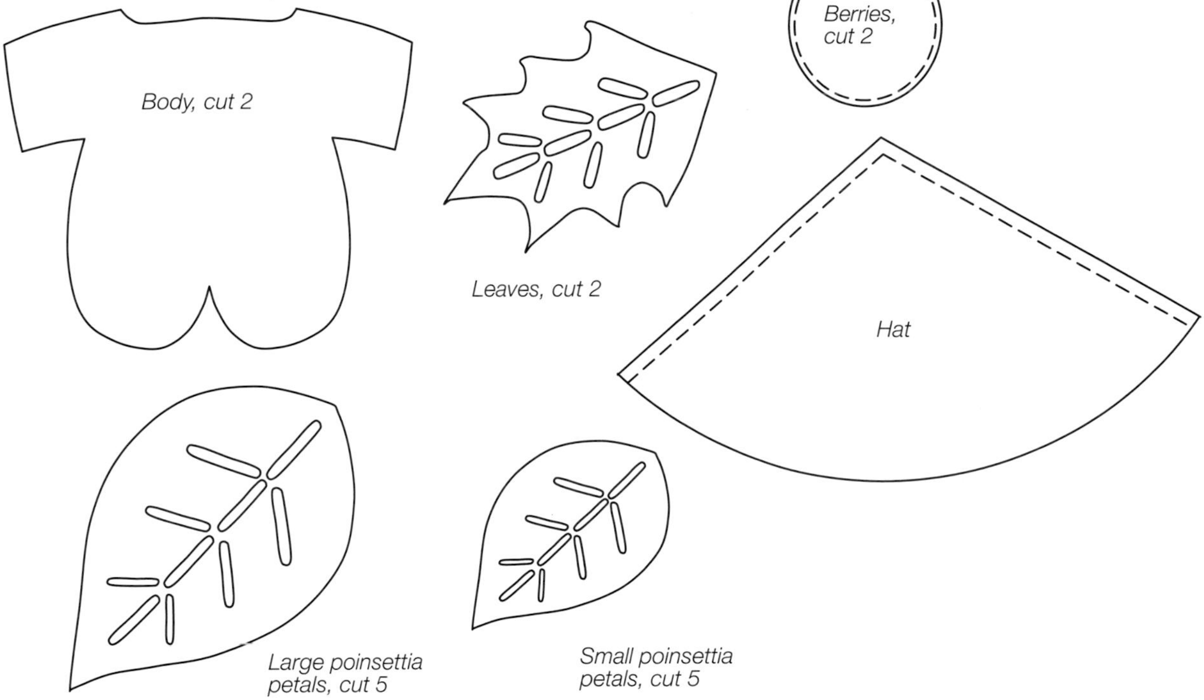

Body, cut 2

Leaves, cut 2

Berries, cut 2

Hat

Large poinsettia petals, cut 5

Small poinsettia petals, cut 5

Mushrooms from the Yule log, page 52

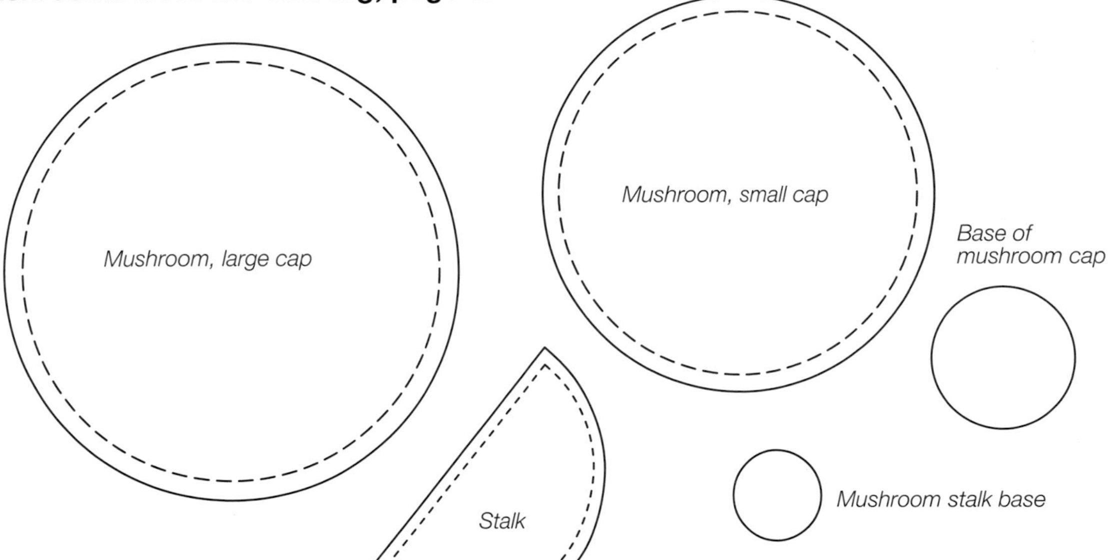

Mushroom, large cap

Mushroom, small cap

Base of mushroom cap

Mushroom stalk base

Stalk

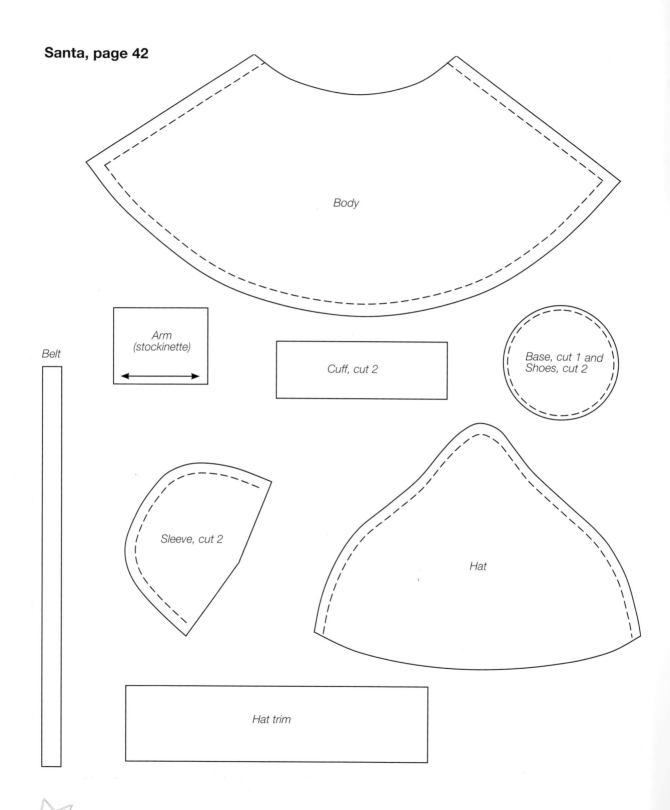

Santa, page 42

Body

Belt

Arm
(stockinette)

Cuff, cut 2

Base, cut 1 and
Shoes, cut 2

Sleeve, cut 2

Hat

Hat trim

Sleigh, page 44

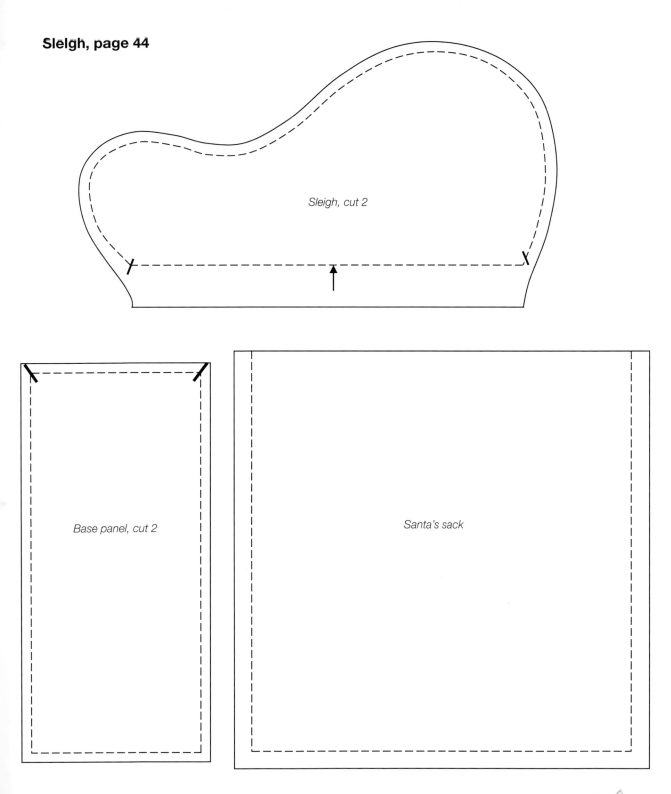

Sleigh, cut 2

Base panel, cut 2

Santa's sack

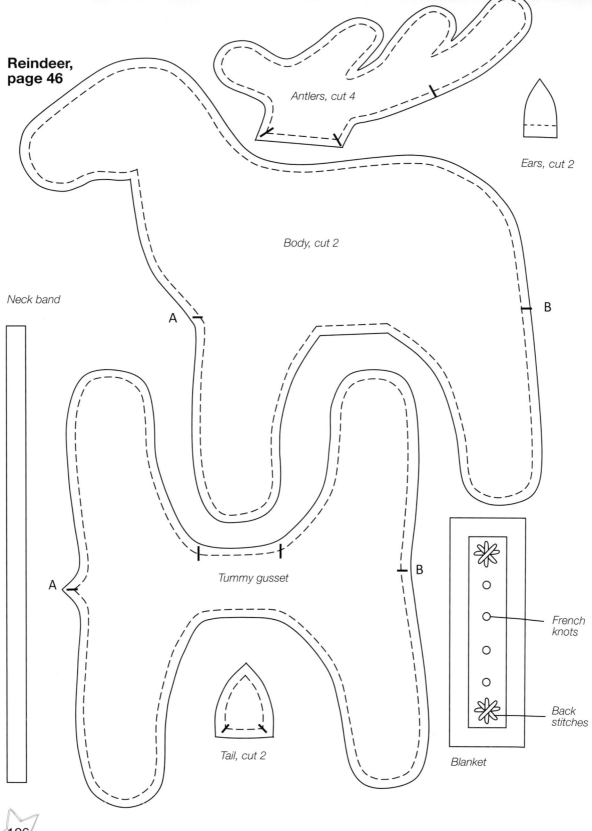

Reindeer, page 46

Antlers, cut 4

Ears, cut 2

Body, cut 2

Neck band

A

B

A

Tummy gusset

B

French knots

Back stitches

Tail, cut 2

Blanket

Yule log, pages 49–53

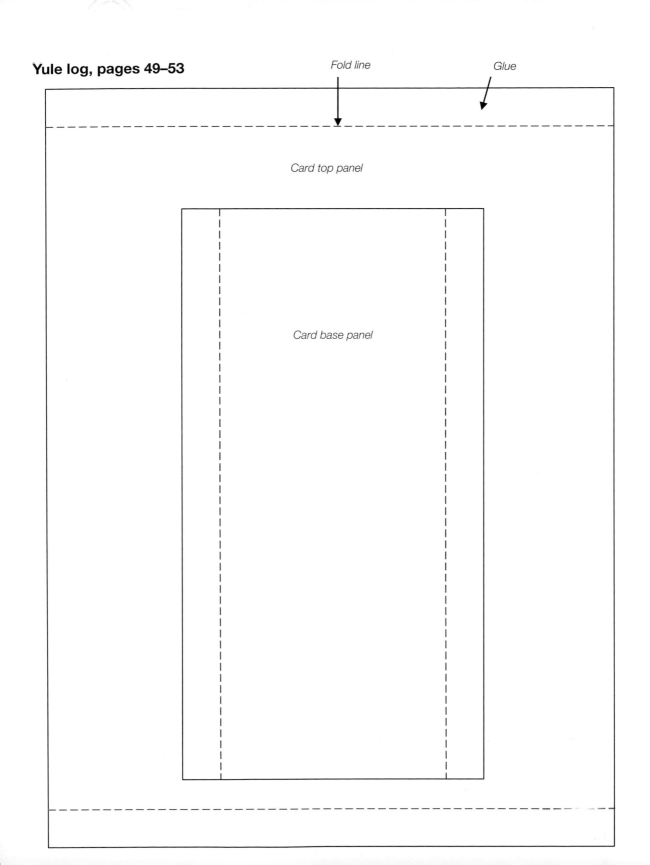

Fold line

Glue

Card top panel

Card base panel

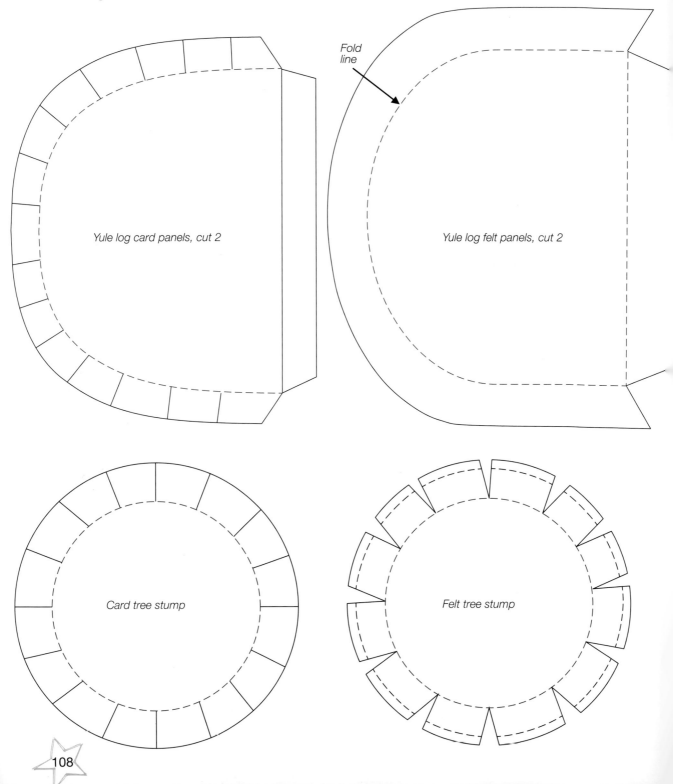

Yule log card panels, cut 2

Fold line

Yule log felt panels, cut 2

Card tree stump

Felt tree stump

Yule log continued

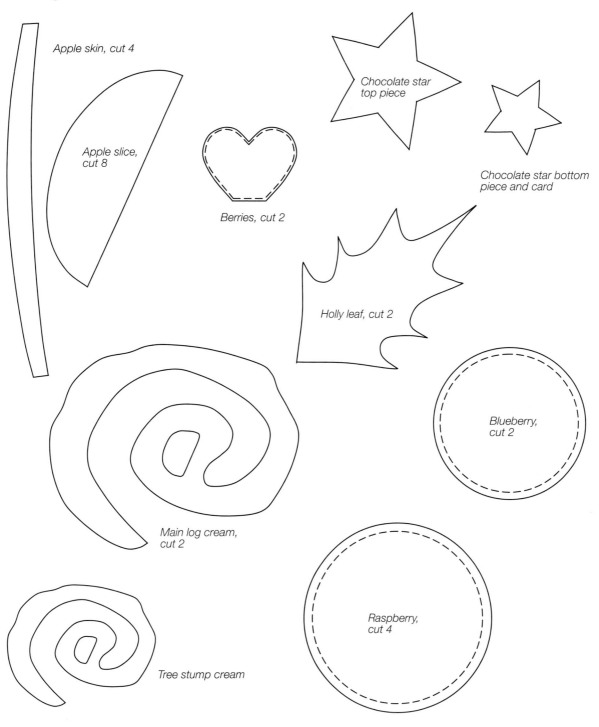

Apple skin, cut 4

Apple slice, cut 8

Berries, cut 2

Chocolate star top piece

Chocolate star bottom piece and card

Holly leaf, cut 2

Blueberry, cut 2

Main log cream, cut 2

Raspberry, cut 4

Tree stump cream

Gingerbread house, pages 56–67

This template is shown half size. Enlarge to 200% before using.

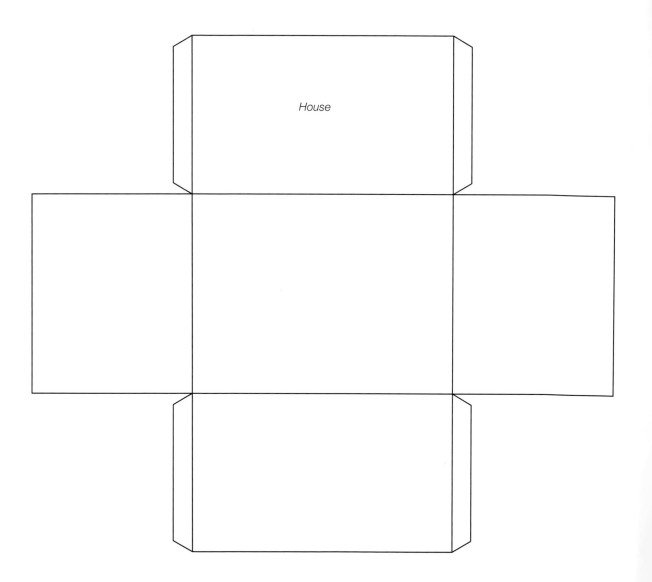

House

Gingerbread house continued

This template is shown half size. Enlarge to 200% before using.

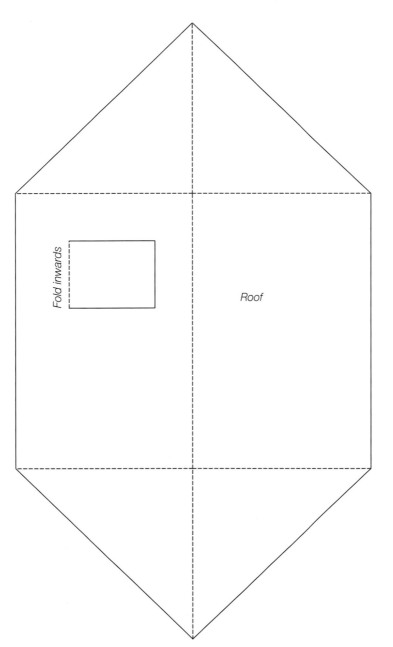

Fold inwards

Roof

Gingerbread house continued

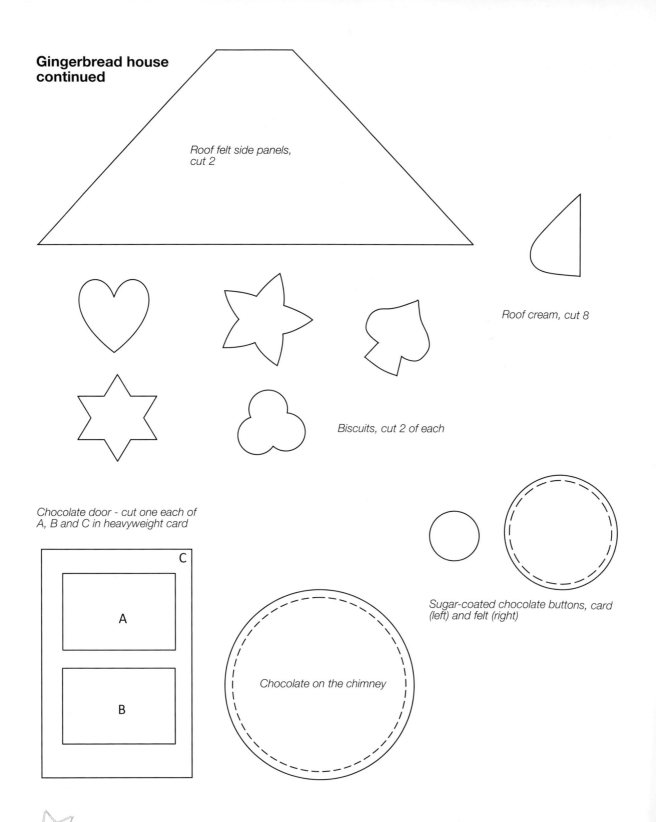

Roof felt side panels, cut 2

Roof cream, cut 8

Biscuits, cut 2 of each

Chocolate door - cut one each of A, B and C in heavyweight card

C

A

B

Chocolate on the chimney

Sugar-coated chocolate buttons, card (left) and felt (right)

Gingerbread house continued

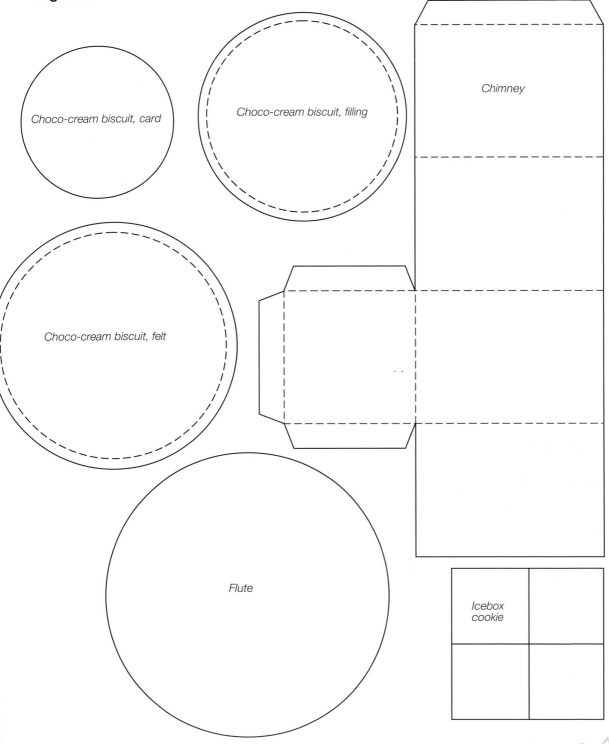

Choco-cream biscuit, card

Choco-cream biscuit, filling

Choco-cream biscuit, felt

Chimney

Flute

Icebox cookie

Gingerbread house continued

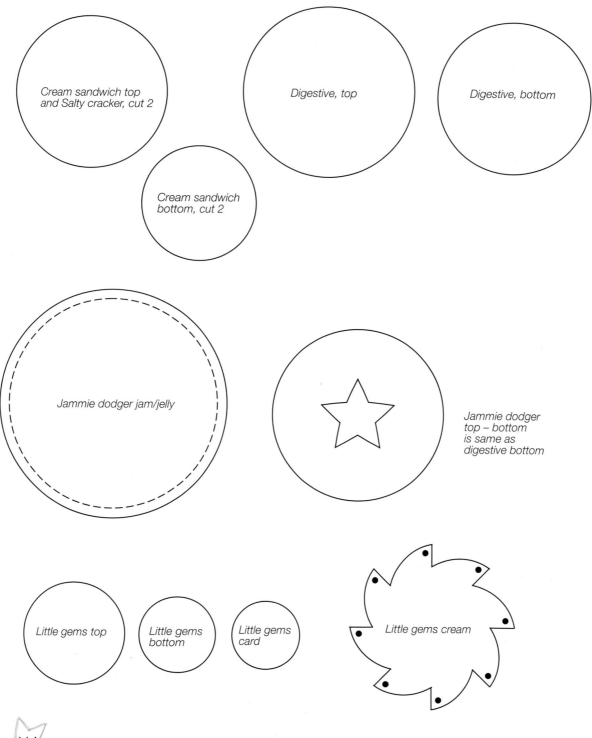

Cream sandwich top
and Salty cracker, cut 2

Digestive, top

Digestive, bottom

Cream sandwich
bottom, cut 2

Jammie dodger jam/jelly

Jammie dodger
top – bottom
is same as
digestive bottom

Little gems top

Little gems
bottom

Little gems
card

Little gems cream

Gingerbread house continued

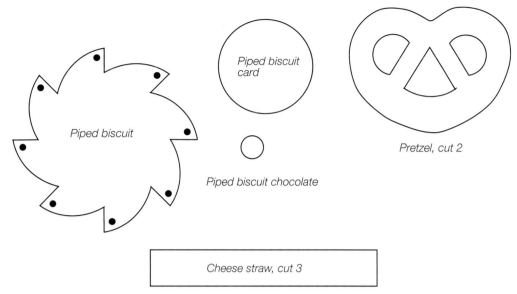

Piped biscuit

Piped biscuit card

Piped biscuit chocolate

Pretzel, cut 2

Cheese straw, cut 3

Fir tree, page 70

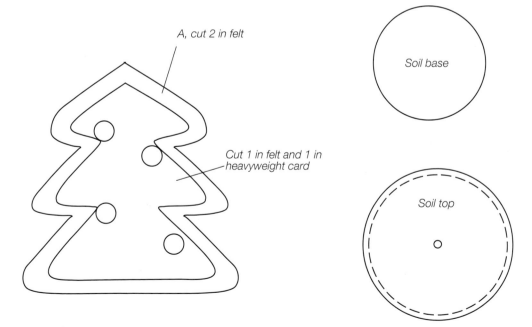

A, cut 2 in felt

Cut 1 in felt and 1 in heavyweight card

Soil base

Soil top

Hansel & Gretel, pages 68–69

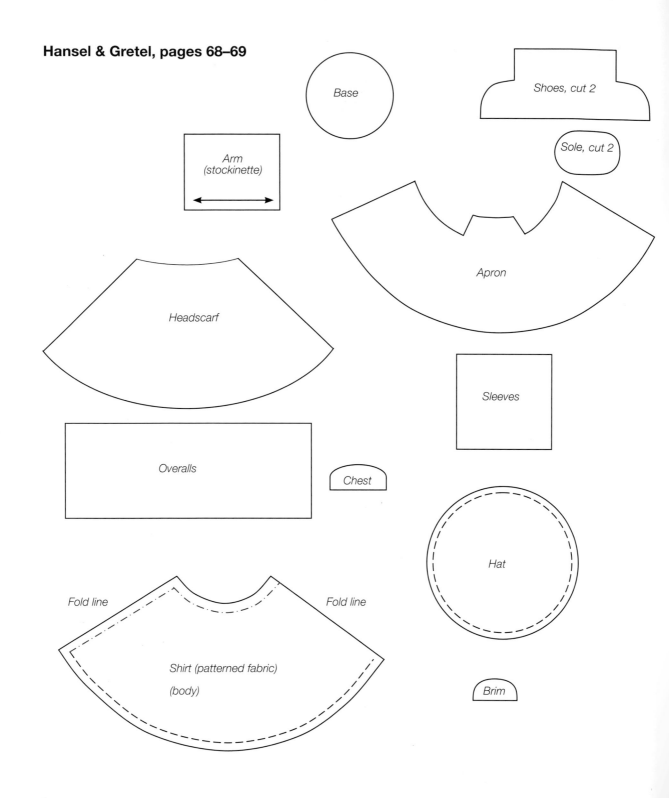

Base

Shoes, cut 2

Sole, cut 2

Arm
(stockinette)

Apron

Headscarf

Sleeves

Overalls

Chest

Hat

Fold line

Fold line

Shirt (patterned fabric)

(body)

Brim

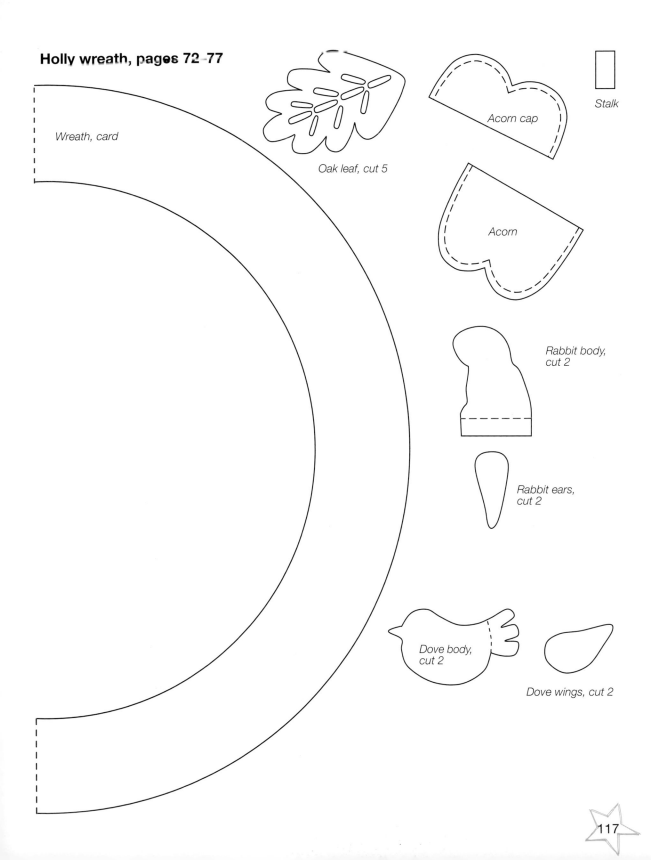

Holly wreath, pages 72–77

Wreath, card

Oak leaf, cut 5

Acorn cap

Stalk

Acorn

Rabbit body, cut 2

Rabbit ears, cut 2

Dove body, cut 2

Dove wings, cut 2

117

Holly wreath, pages 72–77

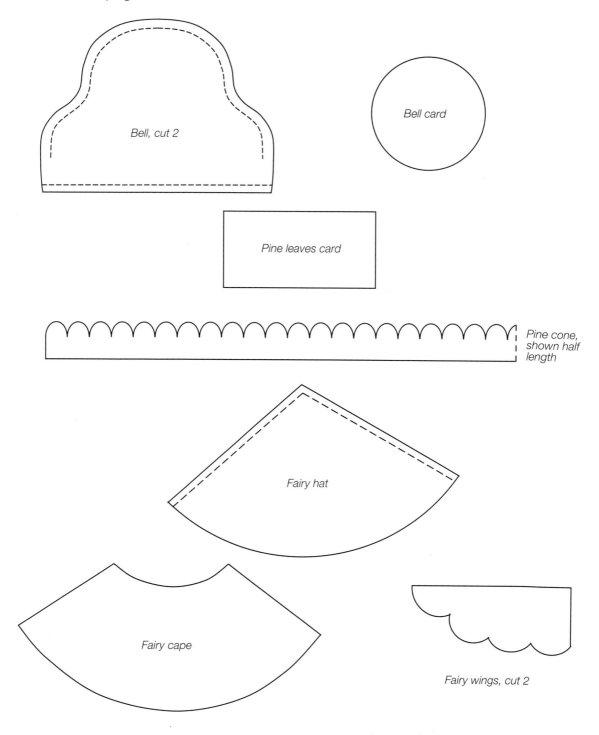

Bell, cut 2

Bell card

Pine leaves card

Pine cone, shown half length

Fairy hat

Fairy cape

Fairy wings, cut 2

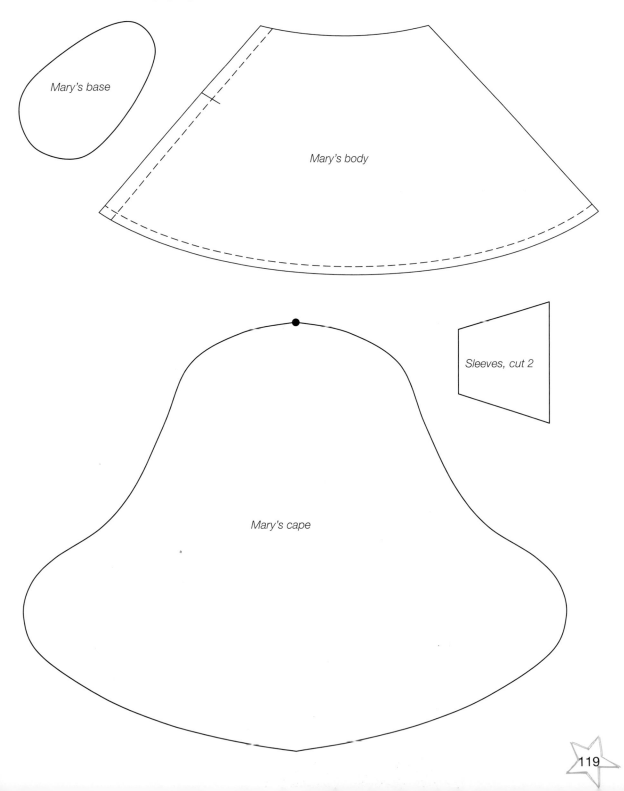

Mary's base

Mary's body

Sleeves, cut 2

Mary's cape

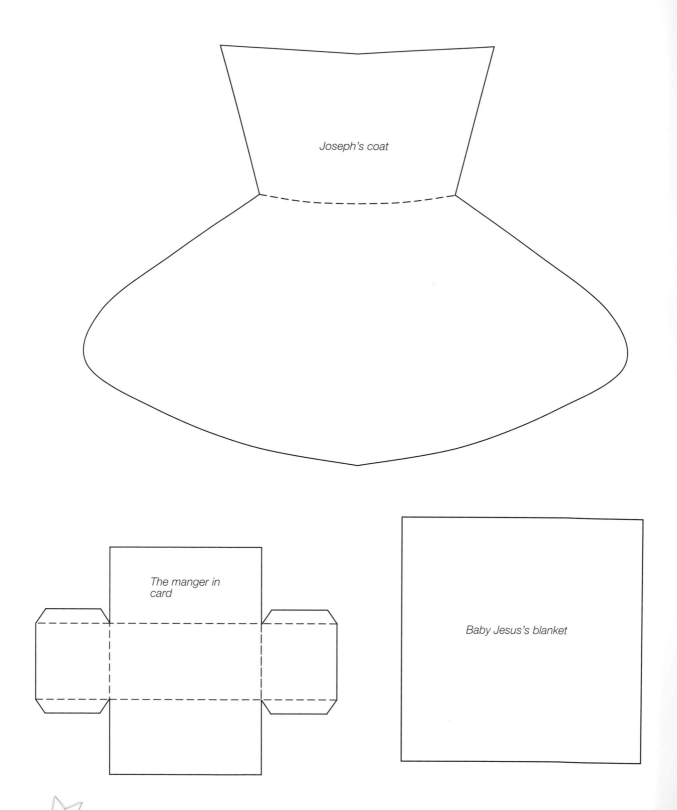

Joseph's coat

The manger in card

Baby Jesus's blanket

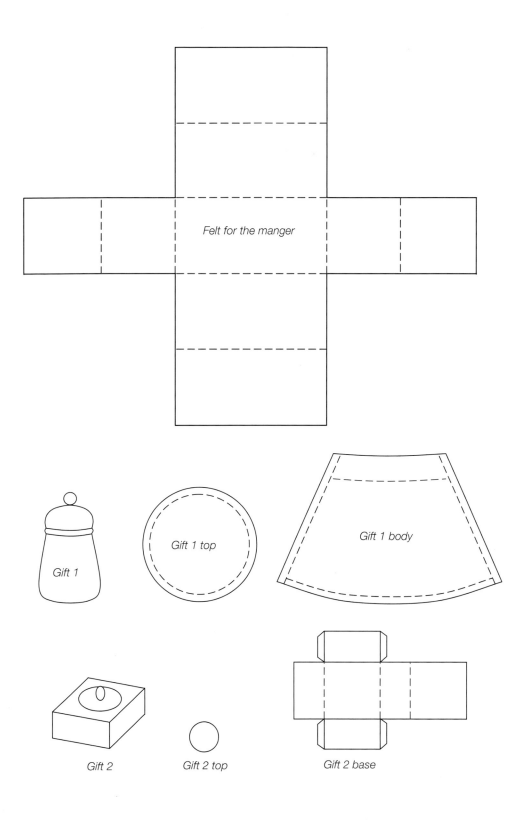

Felt for the manger

Gift 1

Gift 1 top

Gift 1 body

Gift 2

Gift 2 top

Gift 2 base

Gift boxes

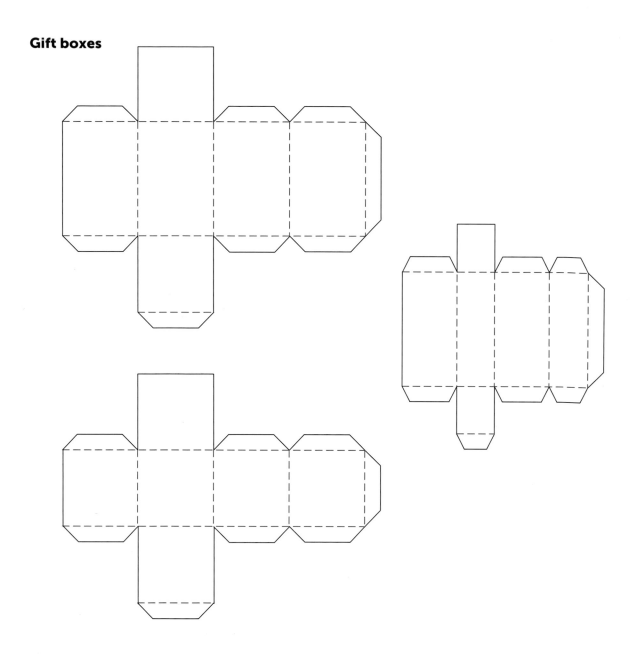

Shepherds

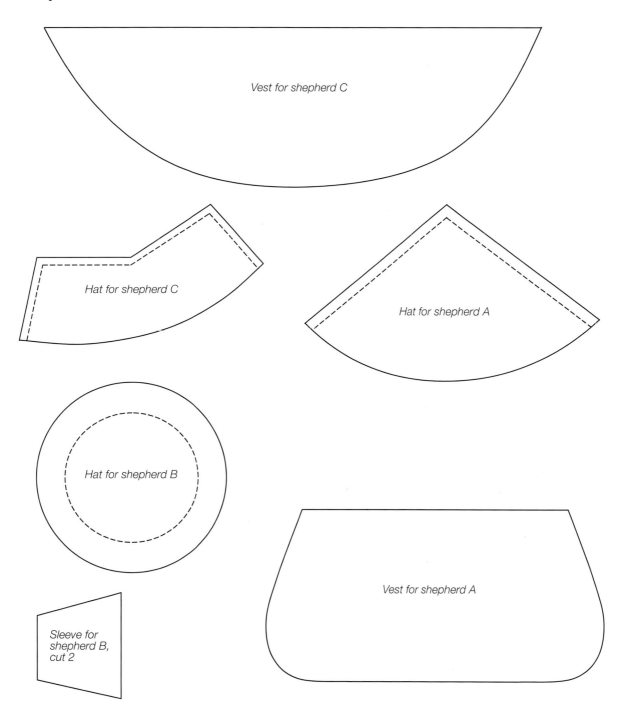

Vest for shepherd C

Hat for shepherd C

Hat for shepherd A

Hat for shepherd B

Vest for shepherd A

Sleeve for shepherd B, cut 2

Kings

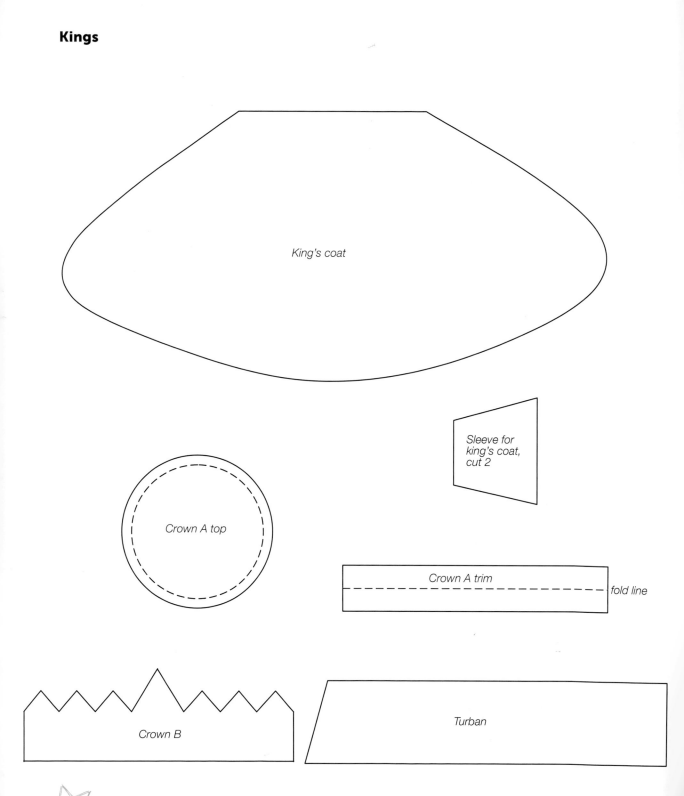

King's coat

Sleeve for king's coat, cut 2

Crown A top

Crown A trim

fold line

Crown B

Turban

Sheep and lamb

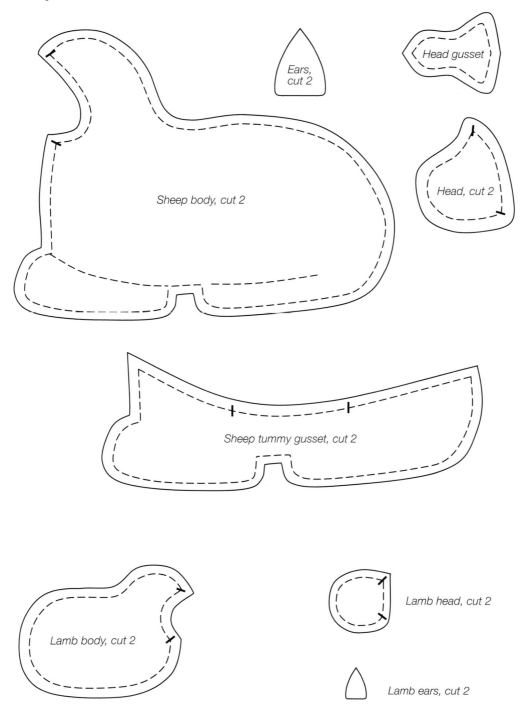

Ears, cut 2

Head gusset

Head, cut 2

Sheep body, cut 2

Sheep tummy gusset, cut 2

Lamb body, cut 2

Lamb head, cut 2

Lamb ears, cut 2

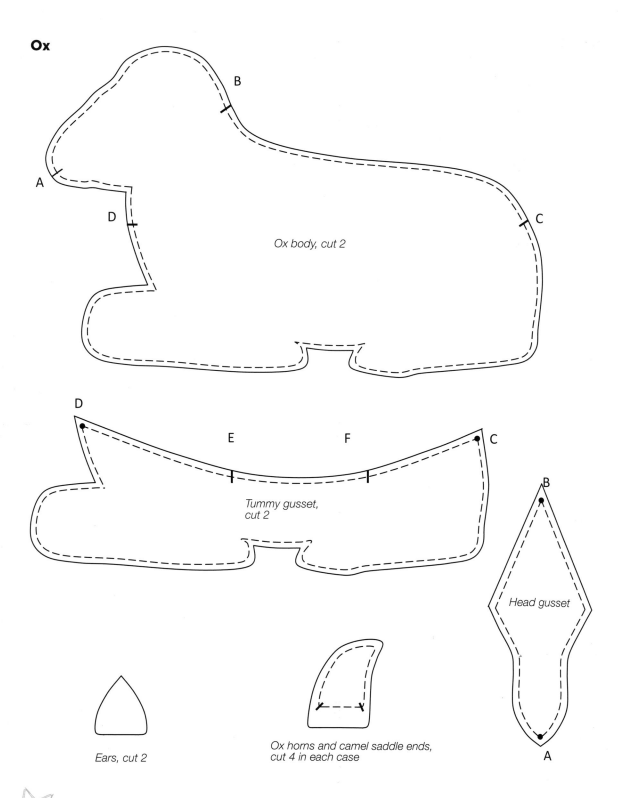

Ox

B

A

D

C

Ox body, cut 2

D

E

F

C

Tummy gusset,
cut 2

B

Head gusset

A

Ears, cut 2

Ox horns and camel saddle ends,
cut 4 in each case

Camels

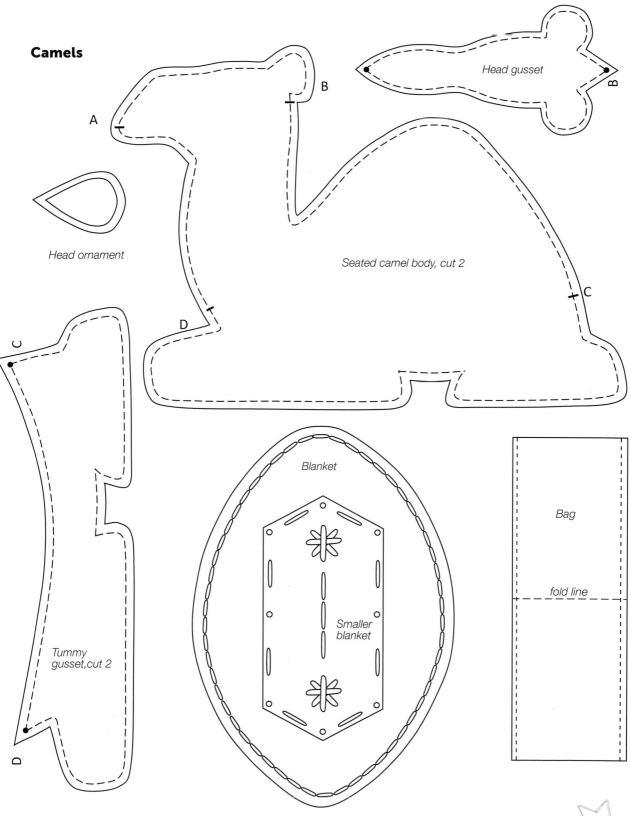

A

B

Head gusset

B

Head ornament

Seated camel body, cut 2

C

D

C

Blanket

D

Smaller blanket

Tummy gusset, cut 2

Bag

fold line

Camels continued

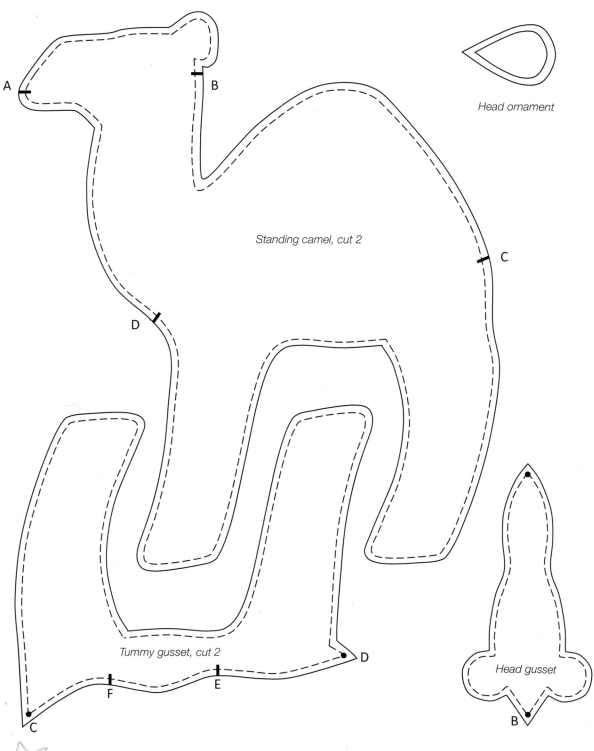

Head ornament

Standing camel, cut 2

A

B

C

D

Tummy gusset, cut 2

F

E

D

C

Head gusset

B